W ithout doubt, meditation is the gateway to the riches of God's revealed truth in the Bible, the *sine qua non* of prosperity and success as God Himself told Joshua. Dr. McIntosh serves in this book as a sure guide to that crucial gateway, thoughtfully escorting the reader to true, biblical meditation in a way that is sensible, insightful (he has well practiced what he preaches!), fascinating, and funny. He demystifies this foundational spiritual tool, stripping away the gauzy haze of pop-philosophies, and showing how it can be used to great spiritual profit by every believer.

> *Rev. Timothy D. Crater*
> ***National Association of Evangelicals***
> ***Washington, DC***

I found my own heart "strangely warmed" as I read his reflections on the power of the Word of God to transform lives. It has motivated me to give more personal time to meditation. I would characterize the book as exhortation, instruction, and illustration regarding the biblical practice of biblical meditation. It's practical, enticing, corrective, and theological. And it's "promising," holding before the reader all that God covenants to give to those who know, believe, and apply the Scriptures. I recommend it for Christians with holes in their souls, which all the movies, sitcoms, and sports fail to fill. Doug gives us a reason to cancel cable and become (re)acquainted with God. There's a bonus for preachers and teachers in all of the valuable illustrations which spice his writing.

It's a book worth meditating on.

> *Johnny V. Miller*
> ***President***
> ***Columbia International University***

HOW TO MEDITATE

ON HIS WORD

God Up Close

Doug McIntosh

MOODY PRESS
CHICAGO

ISBN: 0-8024-7079-3

1 3 5 7 9 10 8 6 4 2

Printed in the United States of America

To my mother,
a peerless encourager
of her children

CONTENTS

MEDITATION CLOSE-UPS

Acknowledgments

W inston Churchill spoke for authors everywhere when he observed that writing a book "is an adventure." As quoted in William Manchester's biography, *The Last Lion, Winston Spencer Churchill,* the statesman, orator, and author elaborated: "To begin with it is a toy and an amusement. Then it becomes a mistress, then it becomes a master, then it becomes a tyrant. The last phase is that just as you are about to be reconciled to your servitude, you kill the monster and fling him to the public." Before I fling this monster toward an unsuspecting public, I cannot fail to express my gratitude to those who helped bring him to life.

I owe a great debt to my colleagues on the board of elders of Stone Mountain Community Church, the body of believers near Atlanta whom I have served since 1971; believing in the book's importance, they granted me a two months' sabbatical to complete the manuscript. Thanks also are due to that patient congregation, who first heard many of the ideas in the pages that follow from their pulpit. SMCC staff members Chuck Taylor and Everett Bracken helped greatly, wedging new responsibilities into already crowded schedules so that I could get away to write.

Special thanks go to Karen Hutto and Carissa McIntosh, who read the manuscript and provided valuable suggestions; to John Haynes, who for years has been encouraging me to put my thoughts on paper; to Emmie Loften, but for whose knowledge of the world of books this one might never have appeared; and to Jim Bell, Jim Vincent, and their colleagues at Moody Press, for sharing my appreciation for the subject. I am also thankful to my wife, Cheryl, upon whose strength, love, counsel, and encouragement I so constantly lean.

I am grateful, too, to Mike and Mimi McClure, dear friends who provided during my sabbatical the use of their lake home in Alabama. That lovely locale proved to be nothing less than a writer's dream environment.

May these encouragements to know God up close prove a blessing in all their lives, and in yours.

A Sure Thing

The wisest of men once remarked that of the making of many books there is no end. You hold in your hand proof that he was right. Nearly three decades of pastoral ministry, nonetheless, have persuaded me that the need exists for at least one more: a volume on the topic of meditation—to be more precise, meditation on the text of Scripture.

The Bible contains remarkable claims of what meditating on God's Word can do for those who practice it. Consider just these four. (Italics have been added to emphasize the claims.)

> This Book of the Law shall not depart from your mouth, but you shall meditate in it day and night, that you may observe to do according to all that is written in it. For then *you will make your way prosperous*, and then *you will have good success.* (Joshua 1:8)

> I have more understanding than all my teachers, for Your testimonies are my meditation. (Psalm 119:99)

I will never forget Your precepts, for by them You have *given me life.* (Psalm 119:93)

Unless Your law had been my delight, *I would then have perished* in my affliction. (Psalm 119:92)

As the psalmist sagely observed, meditation—delighting in God's truth—can make the difference between life and death.

One would think, given the divine source of these grand claims, that people would be climbing all over themselves in their efforts to meditate on the Word of God. Alas, it is not so. Yet having been a Christian believer for forty years I am more convinced than ever that all these biblical claims for meditation—and others yet unmentioned—are valid. Meditation constitutes the single most important activity that any Christian can engage in. Simply put, it works. Meditation is a sure thing.

A sure thing?

Right.

Yes, the expression has been overworked. "A sure thing" has been used in come-ons for real estate scams, personal enrichment tapes, fertilizers, hair dyes, investment schemes, and adhesives. Everybody knows that most of the people who invest in sure things end up sadder, wiser, and poorer (not necessarily in that order).

I don't blame you for being skeptical. I've been taken too— beginning with that advertisement in the back of a comic book when I was eleven years old. "Sell newspapers and win a pony," it read. As a fan of Roy Rogers, king of the cowboys, and his wonder horse, Trigger, I fantasized about riding my soon-to-be-acquired Shetland alongside Roy to capture the bad guys who were terrorizing the beautiful Dale Evans. I decided to go for it. Casting my mother's cautionary words aside, I sent off for my first batch of papers.

After knocking on a couple dozen doors, however, I realized that I'd been had. Even my devilishly cute eleven-year-old charms could not turn my neighbors into readers. So, instead of winning a pony, I was forced to liquidate my few childhood assets to pay for those many papers I could not sell. My newspaper career was over, and Roy lost a promising sidekick.

So I'm skeptical too.

However, God's Book has been tested and found true many times. That might be worth keeping in mind when it comes to exploring meditation's expansive claims. In the chapters that follow, we will look at this ancient and divinely commended practice to discover what it is, how to do it, and the difference it can make. If God's Word can be believed, making meditation a habit will certainly change our lives for the better. If enough people do it, biblical meditation might alter the course of history.

THE NEED OF THE HOUR

As the twentieth century draws to a close, however, biblical meditation has become a strange and unfamiliar practice, even among the people of God. Some have even dabbled in eastern meditation under the mistaken impression that they were engaging in a biblical practice. The most precious commodity ever to be entrusted to humanity, God's inspired Word, still finds many readers, but not nearly enough who meditate upon it. As a pastor, I cringe when I see Clarence Churchgoer's Bible—with his name stamped in gold on its genuine leather cover—sit in our church's lost and found area for weeks at a time. Of course, Clarence *could* be meditating on verses he has memorized. Maybe.

Many western Christians seem to regard the Bible as a classic book—a classic being defined as a volume which people praise and then ignore. Think I'm exaggerating? According to one survey, 68 percent of Americans read the Bible no more than once or twice in a typical week.[1] Since people like to make themselves look good when answering surveys, substituting "month" for "week" might bring us nearer the truth.

Those of us who are evangelicals and like to think of ourselves as "people of the Book" have little room to be smug. Only 22 percent of those who describe themselves as "born again" believers even claim to read the Bible daily, according to the same survey.[2] In the face of verses like, "The testimony of the Lord is sure, making wise the simple" (Psalm 19:7), we stay away in droves. Wisdom is there for the taking, but not enough takers are forthcoming. Pastor Gary Johnson has compiled the distressing data:

The research efforts of Gallup, Barna, and Hunter all indicate that evangelicals are, for the most part, as secular in their orientation as non-Christians. The data reveals, among other things, an astounding degree of theological illiteracy: 84 percent of those who claim the evangelical label embrace the notion that in salvation God helps those who help themselves, 77 percent believe that human beings are basically good and that good people go to heaven regardless of their relationship to Christ, while more than half of those surveyed affirmed self-fulfillment as their first priority. An equal number had a difficult time accepting the concept of absolute truth.[3]

Our simple generation desperately needs divine wisdom. "Simple" is a term often used in Psalms and Proverbs to describe the person without a rudder. He isn't consciously committed to doing wrong, or to anything else for that matter; he simply(!) hasn't a clue about the nature of reality and God's world. He is pushed along by prevailing currents of thought. The Bible insists that the simple person needs God's wisdom, a commodity readily accessible in its pages.

As technology escalates in the modern world, knowledge expands, yet real wisdom becomes correspondingly elusive. We can turn on a personal computer, log onto the Internet, and read words addressed to us only seconds ago from two continents away; we struggle, however, when it comes to making the most basic moral choices—including appropriate ways to use and not to use our personal computers or our television sets.

We have become a generation adrift, with little awareness of God's ways. Not long ago, two men in Boynton Beach, Florida, were arrested and charged with murder and armed robbery. Their motive? To acquire enough money to attend the local police academy—presumably to make south Florida safe from people like themselves. About the same time, a congressman in Honduras was hauled into court by his wife on charges of bigamy. He defended himself by saying "God gave me a physique attractive to women, and I take advantage of it." In our twisted world, God Himself is now to blame for promiscuity.

"Rudderless" isn't a bad adjective to describe the current thinking of the Western world. "Clueless" may be less kind but closer to the mark. G. K. Chesterton once said, "It is often supposed that when people stop believing in God, they believe in nothing. Alas, it is worse than that. When they stop believing in God, they believe in anything."[4] Even public educational institutions offer little in bringing true wisdom to bear on personal morality or public policy. (Significantly, our nation's universities are in the vanguard of disdain for the Scriptures.) One prominent British educator complained (correctly):

> If you want a bomb, the chemist's department will teach you how to make it; if you want a cathedral, the department of architecture will teach you how to build it; if you want a healthy body, the department of physiology and medicine will teach you how to tend it. But when you ask whether and why you should want bombs, or cathedrals, or healthy bodies, the university is dumb and silent. It can help and give guidance in all things subsidiary but not in the attainment of the one thing useful.[5]

LOOKING FOR EXCEPTIONS

These trends may be disturbing, but they hardly justify despair. Rather, they form the ideal setting for the people of God to become incarnate advertising for the gospel of Jesus Christ. The loveliest diamond sparkles most brightly against a dark backdrop.

But is the Christian community an exception to the modern indifference to God's Word? Not a particularly glittering one. In the United States, for example, among those who would describe themselves as born-again Christians, 84 percent think the notion that "God helps those who help themselves" comes from the Bible.[6] It doesn't. (Ben Franklin would be proud.)

The Gallup organization discovered four facts, fascinating in their connection: (1) 82 percent of the American people are willing to describe the Bible as the "literal" or "inspired" Word of God; (2) more than half of America claims to read the Bible at least monthly; (3) half of those people could not name even one of the four gospels; and (4) fewer than half knew who delivered the Sermon on the Mount.[7]

Less than half the adults who attend evangelical churches believe that Satan is a living being, reports researcher George Barna.[8] (The rest generally consider him only a symbol of evil.) After reading the biblical accounts of the temptation of Christ, those of us who have never engaged in an extended conversation with a symbol wonder how it was that the Lord Jesus managed to do so out in the Judean wilderness. Perhaps the event was supposed to be a subtle kind of miracle.

Clearly the modern church has lost its moorings. It has become, to use the Bible's own term, a "simple" church. It means well, but it does not possess the wisdom of God, though most of its members own the Book in which that wisdom is crystallized. We have instead bitten deeply into the world's wisdom. Today, experience and emotions rule. "To thine own emotions be true," we are warned, to paraphrase Browning. To pass up a thrill, even when it comes at the expense of our integrity, is heresy. On the scale of modern sins, denying our emotions fits in somewhere between genocide and pushing elderly ladies in front of trains.

How did we arrive at the current state of affairs? A key reason is the modern church that doesn't read the Bible all that much, hence our warped scale of values. Even more importantly, however, *most of the life-altering power of the Scriptures comes through meditation,* a practice that is only launched when the text is read. As a result of the absence of this process, the Bible does not assume its rightful place as an intimately personal Book, the growth of many Christians is stunted, the church lacks godly servant-leaders, and the gospel suffers from a lack of credibility before the unbelieving world.

FOR THOSE WHO YEARN

The fact that you are interested in meditation enough to have read to this point suggests that you may be an exception, or at least want to be. That's good. The following chapters are written for Christians who are dissatisfied with going through religious motions, who yearn to see the unmistakable evidence of spiritual transformation in themselves, and who want to know how to begin. God's answer is straightforward: meditate on His Word. Meditation *is* a sure thing, because God's truth is sure.

With remarkable benefits coming to those who meditate, one

might expect that ample information would be available about biblical meditation. However, books (good ones, I might add) abound on Bible reading, Bible study, Bible teaching, and Bible interpretation; books on biblical meditation are scarce. Of the 228 book titles listed under "Meditation" in *Books in Print,* only 14 are identifiably Christian in their orientation.[9] Of these, most have little or nothing to do with biblical meditation. Hence, this volume.

As you seek to grow in the practice of meditation in order to better know God and let Him transform you, *God Up Close* can become a helpful companion. Two features of this book will let you review and apply the principles of meditation. "Meditation Close-ups" focus your mind and heart on key ideas in each chapter about God and His working in our lives. "Meditations in His Word" present specific Bible passages on which you can reflect and apply. We hope this book will get you started—or move you further along—in a life of knowing God your Creator.

Our Gracious Queen: To keep your majesty ever mindful of the Law and the Gospel of God as the rule for the whole life and government of Christian princes, we present you with this Book, the most valuable thing that this world affords. Here is wisdom; this is the royal law; these are the lively oracles of God.

—Inscription on the presentation page of the Bible presented to Queen Elizabeth II on the day of her coronation

CHAPTER 1

What Meditation Is

In 1940, an intriguing advertisement appeared in the *New York Times* to promote a forthcoming book. The ad, accompanied by an illustration of a thoughtful young man, read:

HOW TO READ A LOVE LETTER

This young man has just received his first love letter. He may have already read it three or four times, but he is just beginning. To read it as accurately as he would like would require several dictionaries and a good deal of close work with a few experts on etymology and philology.

However, he will do all right without them.

He will ponder over the exact shade of meaning of every word, every comma. She has headed the letter "Dear John." What, he asks himself, is the exact significance of those words? Did she refrain from saying "Dearest" because she was bashful? Would "My Dear" have sounded too formal? . . . Maybe she would have said "Dear So-and-So" to anybody!

A worried frown will now appear on his face. But it disappears as soon as he really gets to thinking about the first sentence. She certainly wouldn't have written *that* to anybody!

And so he works his way through the letter, one moment perched blissfully on a cloud, the next moment huddled miserably behind an eight-ball. It has started a hundred questions in his mind. He could quote it by heart. In fact, he will—to himself—for weeks to come.[1]

The eager and inquisitive spirit of that not-so-fictitious young man (you probably have met a love-struck John) is the fabric of which biblical meditation is made. Meditation is *the adoring believer's interaction with the God of the Bible by means of the Bible.* When I meditate, I engage in three processes:

1. *Realizing* the truth of God as it is contained in the Scriptures. This realization comes from reading and study.

2. *Reflecting* upon that truth, considering its implications for me personally and for the world.

3. *Responding* to God in thanksgiving, worship, and obedience because of that truth.

It should be noted that these processes are not discrete. The person who meditates moves rapidly from one process to the other and back again. As I meditate, I might proceed along these lines:

- I read a portion of the Word.
- I pause to think about it and to consider its application to my heart and experience.
- I become aware during my reflection that I have violated one of God's commandments.
- I respond to God with a confession of my sin.
- I read on, and notice in the text a wonderful example of godly behavior.
- I pause to ask God to help me reflect such character in my own life.
- I read again, and note in the passage a comment on the depth of God's love for me.
- I give Him thanks for that love.

And so on.

"Now wait," you may be saying. "That description matches pretty closely what I have been doing in my 'quiet time' each day. What's the difference?"

Nothing, necessarily. You may have been meditating without being aware of it. On the other hand, a lot of Christians simply read the Bible during their quiet time—if they have one. While there is nothing wrong with just reading a passage of Scripture, meditation as the Bible describes it includes other elements that make more profitable a devotional time alone with God and His Word. Meditation is realizing the truth, reflecting on it, and responding to God on the basis of it.

From this definition we see right away the relationship between reading and study on the one hand and meditation on the other. Meditation includes study, but also forms the connection between Bible study and spiritual living. Meditation cannot be done without study, but study can be done without meditation (as when the student merely looks for answers to specific factual questions, for example).

Recognizing the link between study and meditation, the psalmist asked God for help: "Make me understand the way of Your precepts; so shall I meditate on Your wondrous works" (Psalm 119:27).

This simple prayer reveals a critical principle: Meditation cannot be brought to completion unless there is understanding of God's truth. Neither can it be done without God's assistance. The Spirit of God must illumine the words of the text for there to be understanding.

That does not mean that meditation grinds to a halt at the first interpretive roadblock. So much in the Scriptures is clear that the occasional difficulty is trivial by comparison. The psalmist recognized that in time God could make His precepts plain enough. He prayed, "Open my eyes, that I may see wondrous things from Your law" (Psalm 119:18). If we interact with God on the basis of what is clear, we will have more truth to employ than we can use in a lifetime. Meditation may be slowed down by interpretive difficulties, but it cannot be stopped.

Meditation is likewise incomplete unless it includes an adequate response toward God. It therefore cannot be done in a hurry, perhaps explaining why most people seldom do it on a consistent basis. Psalm 119, the longest chapter in the Bible and devoted to extolling the virtues of meditating on the Word, is also the longest prayer in the Bible. Of its 176 verses, 172 are addressed to God. Meditation may begin in many places, but its end is ever at God's throne.

J. I. Packer's definition of meditation eloquently recognizes these critical points:

> Meditation is the activity of calling to mind, and thinking over, and dwelling on, and applying to oneself, the various things that one knows about the works and ways and purposes and promises of God. It is an activity of holy thought, consciously performed in the presence of God, under the eye of God, by the help of God, as a means of communication with God. Its purpose is to clear one's mental and spiritual vision of God, and to let His truth make its full and proper impact on one's mind and heart. It is a matter of talking to oneself about God and oneself; it is, indeed, often a matter of arguing with oneself, reasoning oneself out of moods of doubt and unbelief into a clear apprehension of God's power and grace. Its effect is ever to humble us, as we contemplate God's greatness and glory, and our own littleness and sinfulness, and to encourage and reassure us— 'comfort' us, in the old, strong, Bible sense of the word—as we contemplate the unsearchable riches of divine mercy displayed in the Lord Jesus Christ.[2]

HAVE YOU GOT THE LOVE?

I have taught on meditation frequently through the years both in church and in the college classroom, and the discussion seldom proceeds for long without someone asking, "How much time will this take?" Teachers love questions like that. One of these days I'm going to respond, "If you have to ask, you can't afford it." Meditation is not one more activity to be wedged into an already overcrowded day. It is the essential lifestyle of the Christian. When will you be finished meditating? When you have no breath left in your body. The psalmist writes, "Oh, how I love Your law! It is my meditation all the day" (Psalm 119:97).

Meditation
Close–up
What *Meditation* Means

Christians often feel confused by, and sometimes even uncomfortable with, the idea of meditation. Part of that may be caused by the mystical purposes associated with eastern religions. So what is biblical meditation? Here are several definitions drawn from this chapter:

- Meditation is the Christian's interaction with the God of the Bible by means of the Bible.
- Biblical meditation consists of a three-part process: (1) realizing the truth of God as it is contained in the Scriptures, (2) reflecting upon that truth, and (3) responding to God in thanksgiving, worship, and obedience.
- Meditation is "the activity of calling to mind, and thinking over, and dwelling on and applying to oneself, the various things that one knows about the works and ways and purposes and promises of God" (J. I. Packer in *Knowing God*).
- Meditation comes from two Hebrew words, *hagah* and *siach*. *Hagah* means to think at length (in order to accomplish some evil objective); *siach* means to reflect or contemplate.
- "Food for my own soul is the object of . . . meditation. The result of this is that there is always a good deal of confession, thanksgiving, supplication, or intercession mingled with my meditation" (George Mueller in *Autobiography of George Mueller*).

The question is not "Do you have the time?" but (to borrow from the shoe commercial) "Have you got the love?" If you have the love, the time will be no problem. If you haven't got the love, you will never take the time. John, our young man who continued to meditate on his 1940 love letter, lost a sense of time as he read and reread the words of his beloved. He had the love.

In his book *The Wonder of the Word of God,* Robert L. Sumner described a Christian man who was severely injured in an explosion. The victim's face was badly disfigured, and he lost his eyesight as well as both hands. As a new Christian, he was distressed to find that he could no longer read the Bible. Hearing about a lady in England who read Braille with her lips, he sent for some books of the Bible in Braille in the hopes he might do the same.

Unfortunately, he discovered in the attempt to learn Braille that the nerve endings in his lips had been destroyed by the explosion. As he brought one of the Braille pages to his mouth, however, his tongue happened to touch a few of the raised characters. The blind man found that he could "read" the Bible using his tongue. Since then, the man has read through the entire Bible four times.[3] That's love.

Moses, too, had the love, and he tried to give it away. Picture in your mind's eye the scene east of the Jordan River fourteen centuries before Christ. Moses is about to go up to Mount Nebo and die, but before he goes to be with God he wants to prepare his people Israel for the greatest test of their young national life.

They are about to cross the Jordan River into the Promised Land to do battle with a series of morally corrupt and belligerent peoples. Israel now must win, by means of conquest, the land God has promised. How will Moses advise them? What will he say to make them equal to the challenges that lie ahead? Will he propose priceless bits of military strategy? Will he have them sharpen their weapons?

Listen to what are nearly the last words of Moses: "Set your hearts on all the words which I testify among you today, which you shall command your children to be careful to observe—all the words of this law. For it is not a futile thing for you, because *it is your life*" (Deuteronomy 32:46–47, italics added).

Christian, set your heart on God's Word—it is your life. God's Word is not simply for regulating your behavior; it is for making you a different kind of person. It is to help you love the right things—including its Author.

You may at the moment lack the passion of the psalmist, who declared: "I opened my mouth and panted, for I longed for Your commandments" (Psalm 119:131). If you find yourself without that burning desire to occupy yourself with God's truth, tell Him so; and ask that He kindle such an affection in you. That is not a request He is likely to deny.

Remember, too, that the psalmist also said: "Consider how I love Your precepts; revive me, O Lord, according to Your lovingkindness" (119:159). Even the most godly need reviving from time to time.

It is devotion that brings changes in the Christian life. George Washington Carver labored for years to explore the values of the peanut. As a result of countless hours of painstaking experiments, he discovered more than 150 products that could be drawn from that lowly plant and revolutionized the economy of the South in the process. When asked how he accomplished so much with the peanut, he replied in words whose application to meditation is obvious: "Anything will yield its secrets if you love it enough."

YOUR LIPS ARE MOVING

When "meditate" appears in the text of the Old Testament, it generally translates one of two Hebrew words: *hagah* or *siach*. These terms overlap a great deal, but each contributes a slightly different spice to God's recipe for meditation.

Hagah literally refers to the making of low or inarticulate sounds. It is sometimes translated *moan,* or *mutter,* and was used of the cooing of a dove (Isaiah 38:14; 59:11) and the growling of a lion (Isaiah 31:4). *Hagah* is often used in reference to the plotting of evil men as they form destructive plans. For example, Psalm 2:1 asks, "Why do the nations rage, and the people plot *[hagah]* a vain thing?"

These verses describe the futility of wicked people who *think at length* of ways to accomplish evil objectives (in this case, the overthrow of God's king). If you are going to kill or rob someone, you have to anticipate all the possibilities: How will you intimidate the victims? What weapons will you have available? How will you carry away the loot? What will be your escape route? Such considerations constitute the "meditations" of evil men.

God wants His people to share such intensity and focus, but to point their meditations in a different direction. The godly person is to lie awake at night thinking of ways to move God's truth into operation in his own life and considering how he can be a blessing to others. This intense preoccupation with thoughts and plans often means that, in meditation, the line between the thoughts and the mouth becomes hazy. The one who meditates is so deeply occupied with his thoughts that his mouth moves without his being aware of it; thoughts spring unconsciously to his tongue.

This may explain the surprising connection between thinking and speaking which occurs in the Bible's first use of *hagah*, Joshua 1:8. There Joshua is told by the Angel of the Lord as he prepares to lead Israel into Canaan, "This Book of the Law shall not depart from your mouth, but you shall meditate in it day and night." Where we might expect to read *mind,* God says *mouth.*

The Lord could be insisting that Joshua's success rests on his calling Israel to accountability to God's Law when he (Joshua) speaks to them. But it is equally possible that he is being told to let his thoughts be so occupied with the Book of the Law that his musings bubble to his lips frequently. It may be unnecessary to choose between these two, since Joshua needed both devotion to the truth and the frequent ministry of it. In any case, "meditation" can refer either to the process of reflection (i.e., thinking) or to the product of it—responses (often verbal) to God on the basis of His truth. Meditation is clearly aloud sometimes, as in: "My mouth shall speak wisdom, and the meditation of my heart shall give understanding" (Psalm 49:3).

The other Hebrew verb that often underlies our English word "meditate," *siach,* means to reflect or contemplate, either internally or audibly ("think out loud"). When the latter is meant, the word is often translated "talk." When the object of the contemplation is painful, "complain" sometimes appears in English translations instead. *Siach* appears in passages like Psalm 77:3: "I remembered God, and was troubled; I complained *[siach],* and my spirit was overwhelmed."

Meditation calls for honesty. If events trouble you, there is nothing wrong with expressing your distress to God (the Psalms are filled with such statements), always within the bounds of reverence. It makes no sense to pretend that you are untroubled anyway. God already knows what is on your mind.

THE COMPANIONS OF MEDITATION

The Psalms subtly teach other aspects of meditation through the parallelism of Hebrew poetry. English and Hebrew verse are often based on the symmetry of paired lines. English poetry often rhymes by means of sounds and/or meter:

> In fourteen hundred and ninety-two
> Columbus sailed the ocean blue.

Hebrew poetry expresses its parallelism instead in terms of *ideas,* often with one line echoing or elaborating on the other:

> The earth is the Lord's, and all its fullness,
> The world and those who dwell therein (Psalm 24:1).

Those words that are used in parallel with "meditate" in the Psalms aid our understanding of what a person who meditates actually does. For example, two companions of meditation are presented in Psalm 143:5: "I *remember* the days of old; I meditate on all Your works; I *muse* on the work of Your hands" (italics added).

Looking back at how God treated His people in the past fortified the psalmist for his own future. Meditation involves reflection: remembering how God has displayed His kindness to you or to others. (The Scripture text provides countless examples of such food for the soul for those whose memory is foggy or whose experience is limited.)

Another companion of "meditate" in the Psalms is one of the most important: "But his *delight* is in the law of the Lord, and in His law he meditates day and night" (Psalm 1:2, italics added).

Meditation is not a casual activity. Only those who esteem ("delight in") the Word will spend the time and energy required to mine its treasures.

HOW GEORGE DID IT

Meditation is something that the serious Christian must do all the time, because it is the key to the heart's condition all during the day. Many have learned this lesson through the years; some because they discovered it in the Bible, others through trial and error. George Mueller, who was one of the latter, was famous for establishing orphanages in England and for joyfully depending on God for all his and his ministry's needs.

How did he maintain such a vigorous faith? He reported in his *Autobiography* how he made a life-changing breakthrough early in his ministry. I quote his description at length both for its detail and to display his enthusiasm for meditation.

> While I was staying at Nailsworth, it pleased the Lord to teach me a truth, irrespective of human instrumentality, as far as I know, the benefit of which I have not lost, though now more than forty years have since passed away. . . .
>
> I saw more clearly than ever that the first great and primary business to which I ought to attend every day was to have my soul happy in the Lord. The first thing to be concerned about was not, how much I might serve the Lord, how I might glorify the Lord; but how I might get my soul into a happy state, and how my inner man might be nourished.
>
> Before this time my practice had been, at least for ten years previously, as an habitual thing, to give myself to prayer, after having dressed in the morning. Now I saw, that the most important thing I had to do was to give myself to the reading of the Word of God and to meditation on it, that thus my heart might be comforted, encouraged, warned, reproved, instructed; and that thus, whilst meditating, my heart might be brought into [an experiential] communion with the Lord. I began therefore, to meditate on the New Testament, from the beginning, early in the morning.
>
> The first thing I did, after having asked in a few words the Lord's blessing upon His precious Word, was to begin to meditate on the Word of God; searching, as it were, into every verse, to get blessing out of it; not for the sake of the public ministry of the Word; not for the sake of preaching on what I had meditated upon; but for the sake of obtaining food for my own soul. The result I have found to be almost invariably this, that after a very few minutes my soul has been led to confession, or to thanksgiving, or to intercession, or to supplication; so that though I did not, as it were, give myself to prayer, but

to meditation, yet it turned almost immediately more or less into prayer.

When thus I have been for awhile making confession, or intercession, or supplication, or have given thanks, I go on to the next words or verse, turning all, as I go on, into prayer for myself or others, as the Word may lead to it; but still continually keeping before me, that food for my own soul is the object of my meditation. The result of this is that there is always a good deal of confession, thanksgiving, supplication, or intercession mingled with my meditation, and that my inner man almost invariably is even sensibly nourished and strengthened and that by breakfast time, with rare exceptions, I am in a peaceful if not happy state of heart. Thus also the Lord is pleased to communicate unto me that which, very soon after, I have found to become food for other believers, though it was not for the sake of the public ministry of the Word that I gave myself to meditation, but for the profit of my own inner man.

The difference between my former practice and my present one is this. Formerly, when I rose, I began to pray as soon as possible, and generally spent all my time till breakfast in prayer, or almost all the time. At all events, I almost invariably began with prayer. But what was the result? I often spent a quarter of an hour, or half an hour, or even an hour on my knees, before being conscious to myself of having derived comfort, encouragement, humbling of soul, etc.; and often after having suffered much from wandering of mind for the first ten minutes, or a quarter of an hour, or even half an hour, I only then began really to pray.

I scarcely ever suffer now in this way. For my heart is being nourished by the truth, being brought into experimental fellowship with God, I speak to my Father, and to my Friend (vile though I am, and unworthy of it!) about the things that He has brought before me in His precious Word.

It often now astonishes me that I did not sooner see this. In no book did I ever read about it. No public ministry ever brought the matter before me. No private intercourse with a brother stirred me up to this matter. And yet now, since God has taught me this point, it is as plain to me as anything, that the first thing the child of God has to do morning by morning is to obtain food for his inner man.

As the outward man is not fit for work for any length of time, except we take food, as this is one of the first things we do in the morning, so it should be with the inner man. We should take food for that, as every one must allow. Now what is the food for the inner man: not prayer, but the Word of God: and here again not the simple reading of the Word of God, so that it only passes through our minds, just as water runs through a pipe, but considering what we read, pondering over it, and applying it to our hearts.

I dwell so particularly on this point because of the immense spiritual profit and refreshment I am conscious of having derived from it myself, and I affectionately and solemnly beseech all my fellow-believers to ponder this matter. By the blessing of God I ascribe to this mode the help and strength which I have had from God to pass in peace through deeper trials in various ways than I ever had before; and after having now above forty years tried this way, I can most fully, in the fear of God, commend it.[4]

God wants His people to be useful to others because they are touched by the joy His Word gives. He wants our ministry to be the overflow of a supernaturally created river of goodness. That beautiful river flows from Himself and is accessible by means of meditation—the adoring believer's interaction with the God of the Bible by means of the Bible.

MEDITATIONS IN HIS WORD

Realize

Read 2 Samuel 22:1–4.

Reflect

1. List the seven or eight terms (actually metaphors) in verses 2–3 that describe God in His relationship to David.

2. Draw lines between the terms which are close synonyms. Where the descriptions are slightly different, how do they differ?

Respond

1. Is there an area of your life where you need to see God act in such ways on your behalf?

2. Are there episodes in your past in which you have seen God defend you? Think about someone who could be encouraged or drawn to the Savior by knowing about them.

3. Turn these verses into a personal prayer by re-wording the text where necessary. Even if you can't honestly pray as David did, you can give thanks for what God has done for you and ask Him to show Himself strong for you in your present circumstances.

The whole counsel of God, concerning all things necessary for his own glory, man's salvation, faith, and life, is either expressly set down in Scripture, or by good and necessary consequence may be deduced from Scripture: unto which nothing at any time is to be added, whether by new revelations of the Spirit, or traditions of men.

—The Westminster Confession of Faith (1646)

CHAPTER 2

What Meditation Isn't

A seminary student in a preaching course once turned in a carefully typed sermon manuscript to his homiletics professor for grading. When the professor met with him to go over the results, the teacher began positively. (He was experienced at dealing with the tender psyches of budding preachers.)

"Your exegesis was well done. You presented the meaning of the text in a helpful and clear fashion. Your three points make sense; they show balance and progression. Your introduction and your conclusion both exhibit a great deal of thought, and the illustrations you used seemed appropriate. However, I am going to give you a D on the sermon."

The student was shocked, as you might imagine. He asked, "Why give me a D if it's all so good?"

The professor said, "Frankly, it's because of your sermon title. It is one of the worst I've ever seen. Nobody will want to come to hear a sermon entitled: 'The Theology of Jesus Examined in the Light of the Eschatology of the Pauline Corpus.' But you can do better, so see if you can come up with a better sermon title and I'll reconsider the grade. What you want is a title that will reach out and grab people by the heart, a title that will compel them to come and hear what you have to say.

"Imagine the sermon title out on the sign in front of a church. What it says should have such impact that if a bus stopped in front of the church and the people on the bus saw the sign, the title would motivate them to immediately get off the bus and run into the church."

The student said that he would give it his best shot. He went home and wrestled with his task all night long, recalling the professor's instructions, and sweating bullets. The next morning he showed up at his prof's office and handed him his sermon, complete with its revised title: "Your Bus Has a Bomb on It!"[1]

Titles can be confusing. All that is *called* meditation today is not identical with what the Bible describes.

EASTERN MEDITATION

In particular, biblical meditation and meditation as practiced in eastern religions (including the New Age movement) use the same name, but are poles apart.

Different in Content

The most critical difference between the two is that eastern meditation empties the mind, while biblical meditation fills the mind with God's Word. In eastern meditation, a guru provides his pupil with a single word, a *mantra,* which is then chanted over and over to rid the mind of conscious thought. Transcendental meditation, a thinly veiled variant of Hinduism made "western" by clever gurus and popularized by the Beatles, claimed during its heyday to be able to cure almost any problem. Its leading proponent in the West advertised that he could tame our violent country, empty America's prisons, and make inmates productive members of society—for a fee—by training people to empty their minds.

Biblical meditation focuses instead on content—God's truth. For example, Psalm 119:48 shows where the writer's attention was aimed: "My hands also I will lift up to your command, which I love, and I meditate on your decrees." Eastern meditation differs from biblical meditation in other ways too.

Different in Design

Eastern meditation is a tool for getting what I want; biblical meditation helps me to want what God wants. In eastern thought, visualizing what I desire is the first step toward getting it. After all, since I am one with the godhead, I can write my own ticket (or so goes the propaganda). Biblical meditation, by contrast, is at least in part a form of prayer, a means of communicating with the God who is separate from the world and who holds everything in the palm of His hand. In Psalm 64:1, the psalmist prayed, "Hear my voice, O God, in my meditation; preserve my life from fear of the enemy."

"Visualizing," a term dripping with New Age overtones and which has been baptized into the Christian faith without benefit of conversion, suggests that reality is what you make it. Biblical meditation, by contrast, requires that we recognize God's transcendence over the world and our individual lives. Reality is what He makes it and how His Word describes it.

Different in Assets

Eastern meditation seeks the ultimate resources that lie within a person. Biblical meditation contemplates the nature of God—not a self-created deity who is within or somehow identical to me (shiver), but the God of the Bible, who alone possesses ultimate power. One best-selling volume on eastern meditation was touted this way: "If you are looking for a way to connect with your inner self, look no further." I have connected with my inner self on several occasions. Frankly, I'd rather not repeat the experience. Apart from the life that Jesus Christ implanted many years ago, there's not much inside me that I can commend.

Christians need contact with the living God, not their inner selves. We are not to deny unpleasant inner realities to which the Bible and our experience alert us, but both doctrine and experience teach us that redemption comes from resources made available to us by God—not from within. "Tapping our resources" only serves to call attention to our innate spiritual bankruptcy.

RECEIVING DIRECT REVELATION

A more subtle error about meditation has crept into the

church in recent years, however. I refer to the fashionable tendency to see ourselves as direct recipients of personalized revelation rather than being people who meditate on a common faith "once for all delivered to the saints" (Jude 3). "Prophets" are increasing in number at the very time in which fewer and fewer Christians make the Book produced by the ancient prophets a part of their daily agenda.

Too many evangelical descriptions of meditation define it (either openly or by implication) as receiving truth directly from God instead of through the Scriptures. An all too typical example: the chapter entitled "The Discipline of Meditation" in Richard Foster's *Celebration of Discipline*.

There is a great deal to commend in Foster's book on disciplines for godly living. His description of meditation, however, is terribly misleading.

For example, Foster describes meditation as a "way of listening to God."[2] He suggests that the Apostle John, "in the Spirit on the Lord's Day" (Revelation 1:10), received truth from God not because he was a prophet favored with the special privilege of being a vehicle for God's Word, but because he had "mastered a way of listening and seeing that we have forgotten."[3]

The recovery of such skills is within reach of all, apparently. For example, Foster says that God will give personalized "instruction on how to relate to your wife or husband, on how to deal with this sensitive problem or that business situation. More than once I have received guidance on what attitude to have when lecturing in a college classroom."[4] All this can be ours if we are "willing to listen." Later, Foster writes that "God is speaking in the continuous present and wants to address us," and he asks believers to reflect on, write down, and interpret their own dreams as a way of learning God's mind. This he calls "unlocking the door to the inner world."[5]

Because Foster sees meditation as primarily a listening activity, it is not surprising that Fosterian meditation moves in some pretty unusual directions. He suggests that we put our imaginations to work and visualize ourselves engaging in some, shall I say, unorthodox activities:

> In your imagination allow your spiritual body, shining with light, to rise out of your physical body. Look back so that you can see your-

Meditation
Close-up
Eastern vs. Biblical Meditation

	Eastern Meditation	**Biblical Meditation**
Mental focus	Empties the mind.	Fills the mind with God's Word.
Content Focus	Asks participants to repeat a single word, a *mantra*.	Asks participants to focus on vital content—God's Word.
Goal	Aids in self-fulfillment.	Aids in honoring God.
Method	Visualizes what you desire.	Prays to God, who controls the universe.
Resources	The ultimate resource is within the person.	The ultimate resource and power is God.

self lying in the grass and reassure your body that you will return momentarily. Imagine your spiritual self, alive and vibrant, rising up through the clouds and into the stratosphere. Observe your physical body, the knoll, and the forest shrink as you leave the earth. Go deeper and deeper into outer space until there is nothing except the warm presence of the eternal Creator. Rest in His presence. Listen quietly, anticipating the unanticipated. Note carefully any instruction given. With time and experience you will be able to distinguish readily between mere human thought that may bubble up to the conscious mind and the True Spirit which inwardly moves upon the heart.[6]

The trip's description continues, but let us exit the spacecraft at this point.

Only our own stubborn unwillingness to listen to God separates us from these blessings, according to Foster. He condemns the Israelites' desire to have Moses act as their mediator on Mount Sinai: "Human beings seem to have a perpetual tendency to have somebody else talk to God for them. We are content to have the message secondhand. At Sinai the people cried out to Moses, 'You speak to us, and we will hear; but let not God speak to us, lest we die.'"[7] In Foster's practice of meditation, the Bible is secondhand stuff, and less desirable than getting one's truth directly from God.

However, his evaluation of the Israelites' reluctance to hear the voice of God is rather different from God's own. As Moses later recalled the people's request at Sinai, "The Lord said to me: 'I have heard the voice of the words of this people which they have spoken to you. *They are right in all that they have spoken. Oh, that they had such a heart in them that they would fear Me and always keep all My commandments, that it might be well with them and with their children forever!*'" (Deuteronomy 5:28–29, italics added).

What Foster sees as evidence of a substandard spirituality, God finds wonderfully refreshing. The Lord knew that the terrifying unveiling of His power and glory at Sinai should have been enough to unsettle anyone. In all the travels of Israel from Egypt to Canaan, their request for Moses to mediate the Word of God is one of the few sensible and commendable requests that they made. It makes sense to have a mediator when God shakes the earth.

The Christian who meditates on the text of Scripture does not come to it because he does not want God to speak, but because he believes God already has spoken. We enter the presence of God to worship on the basis of a completed revelation, not to acquire more of it. Meditation is not seeking after *revelation*, but *illumination*. The difference is critical. Charles Ryrie explains:

> The experience of illumination is not by "direct revelation." The canon is closed. The Spirit illumines the meaning of that closed canon, and He does so through study and meditation. Study employs all the proper tools for ascertaining the meaning of the text. Meditation thinks about the true facts of the text, putting them together into a harmonious whole and applying them to one's own life. The end result of the illumination ministry of the Spirit is to glorify Christ in the life, or to promote healthy doctrine—teaching that

brings spiritual health and wholeness to the believer's life.[8]

The meditating believer does not regard the Bible as second-hand material, a concession extended to spiritual wimps not bold enough to hear from God directly. On the contrary, the Bible constitutes an accurate unveiling of His Person, *given through mediators because of God's loving sensitivity to our condition*. The Bible is thus worthy of all the diligence the believer possesses, precisely because it is the product of God's very breath (the meaning of the word "inspired" in 2 Timothy 3:16–17). He first gives it to us, then serves as our resident Teacher as well.

Former President Ronald Reagan used to love to tell the story (which he insists is true) about the photographer who worked for a Los Angeles newspaper. The man received an urgent call from his boss, instructing him to take some aerial pictures of a fire that was burning out of control in the area of Palos Verdes Estates, a seaside community south of Los Angeles. He was told to proceed immediately to a small airport near the fire where a plane would be standing by, ready to take off.

In accordance with instructions, the photographer shattered most of the local speed laws in route to the airport and found, as he had been told, a small plane waiting with the engines already turning. He quickly climbed aboard, yelled "Let's go!" and at about five thousand feet, began getting his cameras out of the bag. He told the pilot to get him over the fire quickly so he could take his pictures and get back to the newspaper office in time for the afternoon edition. There were several seconds of silence from the pilot. Then came the hesitant question: "Uh ... you aren't the instructor?"

Being sure the Instructor is present is never a problem when you meditate. If you are a Christian believer, He is present with you at all times. He is waiting to meet with you and to have His Word begin the process of bringing you some wonderful benefits. Just make sure your seat belt is securely fastened.

MEDITATIONS IN HIS WORD

Realize

Read Ephesians 4:25–32. Note the link between the negative and positive commands in verse 25: ("put away. . . speak"). How many similar pairs can you find in verses 26 through 32? God apparently thinks that we need both turning away from what is wrong and turning toward what is right. Does such pairing suggest a strategy for defeating long-standing sinful habits?

Reflect

1. Do Christians frequently lie to one another? Did you ever respond to a concerned inquiry about how things were going by denying that you were facing a problem?

2. Is anger always sinful? When does it become sinful?

Respond

1. Is there anyone toward whom you have been holding a grudge—letting "the sun go down on your anger"? What will you do today to change that?

2. The basis of the believer's forgiveness of others is his own forgiveness in Christ (v. 32). Have you been withholding forgiveness from someone by erecting conditions that they must meet in order to merit your forgiveness? What will you do differently now?

3. Offer to God a prayer of thanksgiving for the completeness and unconditionality of your own standing with Him.

If I find in myself a desire which no experience in this world can satisfy, the most probable explanation is that I was made for another world.

—C. S. Lewis

CHAPTER 3

The Motive for Meditation

Two men walked along the dusty Roman road from Jerusalem to their home in the little village of Emmaus. They were not, however, enjoying the spring afternoon; they were talking as people will talk when they are confused and distressed.

Sometimes both spoke at once. Then there were stretches when they fell silent; then one or the other would begin again.

"What do you think it all means?"

"I don't know; I can't discount it. What about the rumors from the women? What about Peter and John and what they saw?"

As they were weighing the stories that had stunned the Holy City, a stranger joined them. Almost at once the stranger inquired about the subject of their discussion.

"It's what everybody in town is talking about today," one replied, "about Jesus, the prophet from Nazareth. He was executed by the Romans on Friday, but there are persistent stories around town that He has been raised from the dead. We don't know what to make of it. We were hoping that He would be the one to redeem Israel—but now, we just don't know."

You may recall the rest of the story (in Luke 24:13–31)—how

the stranger, who seemed to have joined them by chance, rebuked them for their hardness of heart regarding the Scriptures; how He began in Genesis to explain the prophecies to them, demonstrating that it was always in the plans for the Messiah to die for the sins of men; how He was invited in to supper, and how, as He broke bread, He suddenly was recognized as who He really was, the Messiah Jesus Himself. Then, just as quickly, He vanished.

Heads dizzy with excitement, they began to review that remarkable conversation along the road, recalling joyfully, "Did not our heart burn within us while He talked with us on the road, and while He opened the Scriptures to us?" (v. 32). The Lord Jesus joined link after link after link of the prophetic Scriptures to Himself. And then . . . He was gone.

MEDITATION: AN ENCOUNTER WITH THE RISEN LORD

Today, in Jesus' physical absence, He who is the living Word meets believers in the pages of the written Word. Our hearts burn pleasantly as we sense that what we are reading is the truth, given by God for our good. Meditation is the closest we can come today to a face-to-face encounter with the risen Lord Jesus. We should remember that truth as we face the challenge of making time for our daily appointments with Him.

Your motivation—or the lack of it—will determine whether you undertake meditation as the lifelong adventure King David knew it to be. The critical issue in meditation is not time, but love. The sweet psalmist of Israel was not reluctant to express his strong feelings about meditation. He declared his yearning again and again in Psalm 119, for example: "My soul breaks with longing for Your judgments at all times" (v. 20). "I cling to Your testimonies; O Lord, do not put me to shame!" (v. 31). "Behold, I long for Your precepts; revive me in Your righteousness" (v. 40). He knew how utterly valuable God's precepts were, and as a result was willing to pay any price to make them a part of his heart.

Why was David so passionate about God's Word? He knew that meditation was the means of addressing the deepest needs he possessed. That is what makes the practice so critical. That is why David's heart broke with longing for God's commandments, and why he pleaded with God to teach him the Word. Meditation remains God's chosen method of meeting the cravings of our hearts.

THE MOTIVE: A LONGING TO KNOW GOD

There are really two different varieties, if you will, of longings after God. One is the extension of the other. The first variety is one that is universally implanted by God because we are human beings. *He made us to know Him.* He placed man in Paradise, gave him every advantage, and took the initiative to walk and talk with him. Man was complete in those days. He had everything, because he knew God.

After man sinned, he still possessed a longing for God, but God was no longer available. So, he began the painful process of carrying around an emptiness which—for Adam, at least—was an aching he understood. A measure of relief from the implanted longing takes place at conversion. Jesus Christ takes up residence within the heart of the believer at that point.

There is still, however, an extension of the implanted longing. If you want to give it a different name, call this second longing *the longing of experience*—the craving of the believer not simply to be acquainted with God through Christ, but to know Him deeply. David invited us to a royal feast: "Taste and see that the Lord is good; blessed is the man who trusts in Him!" (Psalm 34:8).

The one who has tasted the Lord will verify that He tastes good. He deals with us in such grace, kindness, and faithfulness that once you and I have tasted a little, we want more. A longing for God in this sense is a holy dissatisfaction with one's experience of God—not that what I do know is wrong, but that I desire it to be more complete.

His Word will make it more complete.

Since Adam passed off the scene, people have not only lost the knowledge of God, most have lost the awareness that He is what they are missing. So they go from place to place, from person to person, from activity to activity, looking to fill the void with items that always, in the end, disappoint. Blaise Pascal once noted, "There once was in man a true happiness of which now remain to him only the mark and empty trace, which he in vain tries to fill from all his surroundings, seeking from things absent the help he does not obtain in things present. But these are all inadequate, because the infinite abyss can only be filled by an infinite and immutable object, that is to say, by God Himself."[1]

Pascal pegged each person as "seeking from things absent the help he does not obtain in things present." What we think will fill our longings is whatever we don't have at the moment. What we forget is that five years ago the possession we didn't have but which we were sure would make us happy is what we have six of today. And are we happy? Of course not.

Why don't things satisfy? Why don't achievements satisfy?

Because God won't let them. He knows that the only thing that will ease our ache is to know Him personally. Knowing Him well is the goal of meditation.

A DANGEROUS ILLUSION

You have, I am sure, read passages of Scripture in which God appears to someone and speaks with him directly or performs a mighty miracle. If you are like me, perhaps you found yourself musing, "If I could have been at . . . (the Red Sea, or Jericho, or the raising of Lazarus, or . . . fill in the blank), seeing those remarkable events would have given me so much spiritual certainty and energy I would never need anything else!"

An understandable sentiment. Unfortunately, it is also a misguided one. It is refuted, for one thing, by the experience of Israel during the Exodus. Two million people saw God open the Red Sea and save them while destroying the pursuing Egyptians. Two million people were led by a pillar of fire by night and a cloud by day. Two million people were fed miraculously each morning by God's manna. If wondrous and supernatural experiences could create and sustain godly living, that group of people would have been Israel's most godly.

Yet no generation proved so disappointing. They were so out of touch with spiritual realities that, in the end, God had to lead them around in the Sinai wilderness until they died so that He could make a fresh start with the next generation.

Seeing is not believing. Experiencing miracles can never pro-

Meditation
Close-up
The Longing Heart

Every man and woman has a longing for God. In the Scrip-tures, the idea of the *heart* as the source of our greatest longing takes several forms, and acting upon that longing will bring both rewards and strong opposition:

1. The intelligence and will reside in the heart (see Hebrews 4:12).

2. The heart either inclines toward God or to God's competi-tors—the idols of materialism, self, or other man-centered reli-gions. Our hearts are never neutral, for our wills and desires are not neutral (see Matthew 6:24).

3. God welcomes and rewards those whose hearts pursue Him (see Matthew 5:6).

4. Those who seek strongly after God will face attacks from their emotions, the enemies of God, time constraints, and even from casual Christian friends (see Ezra 6:21).

5. Knowledge of God comes through meditating on His Word and applying it. This means obedience to the Scriptures is crit-ical for our drawing closer to God.

duce lasting spiritual maturity. Peter, for example, knew the limita-tions of observing wonders and of being involved in them. He was privileged, with James and John, to see one of the greatest miracles in human history: The Lord Jesus was transfigured before the three disciples upon a mountain in a preview of the glorious Second Coming. Moses (finally making it to the west side of the Jordan) and Elijah appeared with Him there.

Years later, Peter recalled the event when he wrote, "We did not follow cunningly devised fables when we made known to you the power and coming of our Lord Jesus Christ, but were eyewitnesses of His majesty" (2 Peter 1:16). He identified the Transfiguration as a visual prefiguring of the Second Coming.

Peter did not say, however, that Christ's followers could rely on the certainty of the Second Coming because he witnessed a miracle that foretold it. On the contrary, he established the priority of Scripture by writing, "We also have the prophetic word made more sure, which you do well to heed as a light that shines in a dark place" (v. 19). The value of the Transfiguration was that it confirmed "the prophetic word." Experiences fade with the years; God's Word never changes. It is in that Word, not in the memory of a miracle, that we meet the One we need. We have to incline our hearts to seek Him there.

THE LEANING HEART

As he was about to pass off the scene, Joshua called Israel to a solemn assembly at Shechem. There he reviewed how God had brought them into possession of the land and vanquished their enemies. Then he called on them to choose their loyalties: "Choose for yourselves this day whom you will serve, whether the gods which your fathers served that were on the other side of the River, or the gods of the Amorites, in whose land you dwell. But as for me and my house, we will serve the Lord" (Joshua 24:15).

The people's response would have cheered the heart of most preachers. They said, "We also will serve the Lord, for He is our God" (v. 18).

Joshua, however, was not most preachers. He brought them up short when he said, "You cannot serve the Lord, for He is a holy God. He is a jealous God; He will not forgive your transgressions nor your sins" (v. 19). Joshua insisted that they realize that the God of heaven is not like pagan deities that don't even exist. If you make a covenant with God, Joshua insisted, be prepared to follow through. The people insisted that such was their intention, whereupon Joshua commanded them, "Put away the foreign gods which are among you, and incline your heart to the Lord God of Israel" (v. 23).

That's exactly what we need: a heart leaning in God's direction. That will get us started.

A Definition

In the English language, the *heart* is usually understood as the seat of the emotions or convictions. In the language and culture of the Scriptures, however, the "heart" is the place where two functions coincide: the intelligence and the will. The classic verse on the subject, Hebrews 4:12, says, "The word of God is living and powerful, and sharper than any two-edged sword, piercing even to the division of soul and spirit, and of joints and marrow, and is a discerner of the thoughts and intents of the heart." Note that final phrase: *The thoughts [of the heart]*—the heart is the locus of intelligence; *and the intents of the heart*—the heart is the seat of the will.

From the biblical point of view, the two go together. You cannot decide on a course of action without being aware of the options. On the other hand, it makes no sense to know the truth and then decide to do what you know to be false or useless. The mind is not the enemy of the will, but its necessary ally. It is the will that chooses to seek the Lord; it is the mind that makes sure that it is the God of the Bible who is being sought.

Tilting in the Right Direction

Joshua knew that his brethren could incline their hearts if they chose to do so. There is no point in commanding someone to do what is impossible. They could incline their hearts toward God, and so can we.

I have to hedge a little here and note that inclining the heart is possible most of the time, but at times we can lose that ability or at least have it compromised. Consider David's prayer in Psalm 119:36, "Incline my heart to Your testimonies, and not to covetousness." There wouldn't be much of a point to that request if inclining the heart were totally an ability the person possessed. David recognized that even as he spoke he could easily wander away and follow the natural inclinations of his heart into covetousness and materialism. His prayer reflects an awareness of the special temptations faced by a king.

For the most part, however, God expects us to take responsibility for the direction in which our hearts are inclined.

Always Tilted

The neutral heart is nowhere to be found. We are always inclined in one direction or another. Joshua wisely linked inclining the heart toward God with putting away the foreign gods of Israel. He knew that the people would never incline their hearts to God as long as they were harboring His competition. Foreign deities eventually would become the downfall of God's ancient nation and cause God to send them into exile.

The direction and tilt of our hearts is the product of our inner life: the way we think, the things we choose to love, and the purity of our intentions. Jesus said, "No one can serve two masters" (Matthew 6:24). Meditation will never coexist with impurity or covetousness. God's Word will drive out the sins, or those sins will drive you away from God's Word.

THE SEEKING HEART

"Seeking the Lord," a more intense way of describing what believers can do, may be defined as refusing to allow one's relationship with the true and living God to remain static. In positive terms, it means pursuing a knowledge of God as far as you can. How far can you pursue knowledge? Infinitely far. After all, the Scriptures teach that God is an infinite Person. His depths cannot be fully plumbed: "Oh, the depth of the riches both of the wisdom and knowledge of God! How unsearchable are His judgments and His ways past finding out!" (Romans 11:33).

Becoming a Christian is crucial but marks only the beginning of a lifelong process of seeking Him. Conversion gives you the spiritual equipment to engage in a quest that will last not only throughout your earthly life, but through eternity itself.

During an interview with a group of astronauts, the crew members were asked, "What do you think is the single most important key to successful space travel?" One astronaut offered the following response: "The secret of traveling in space is to take your own atmosphere with you." That is what it takes to seek God. You take your atmosphere—God's Word—with you wherever you go. You recognize that there is more of God to know, and you are determined to know all of Him you can.

If you set your heart to seek God, if you really want to know Him and you tell Him that, do you think He will turn you down? Not a chance. "Blessed are those who hunger and thirst for righteousness, for they shall be filled" (Matthew 5:6). This pursuit is what He made you for. He is not going to play hide-and-seek with you. But you have to want to know Him.

During the rule of King Asa of Judah, the nation had sunk into a moral hole. Meanwhile—and clearly related to the people's rebellion against God—foreign armies threatened the national borders. In His grace, though, God sent a prophet to urge the people to move in a new direction. Second Chronicles 15 records what happened; it represented a complete about-face as they longed not for themselves but for God:

> Then they entered into a covenant to seek the Lord God of their fathers with all their heart and with all their soul; and whoever would not seek the Lord God of Israel was to be put to death, whether small or great, whether man or woman. Then they took an oath before the Lord. . . . And all Judah rejoiced at the oath, for they had sworn with all their heart and sought Him with all their soul; and He was found by them, and the Lord gave them rest all around. (2 Chronicles 15:12–15)

Notice, the oath was based on *a total commitment* and was publicly enforceable. People could tell by what an individual did whether he was truly seeking the Lord. No one in Jerusalem, for example, who built a shrine for a pagan god could have been seeking the Lord.

Now you may think, "I'm not sure I would want to live in a society where failure to seek God was a capital offense." I understand that. But the covenant was voluntary, and the outcome of it—at least for a brief period of time—was that "He was found by them, and the Lord gave them rest all around." Their society became peaceful and prosperous because of their corporate commitment to seeking Him.

So how do you go about seeking the Lord?

Making Up One's Mind

"Even the journey of a thousand miles begins with a single step," the Chinese proverb says. It is that way too when seeking the Lord. The people of Judah recognized that they would have to display an iron determination if they were to seek God successfully. They did it and so can we. The text of Scripture is where God waits to be found. Meditation is the vehicle by which it can be done.

What is to keep you from seeking Him? Everything. Everything in human experience works against you on this sin-cursed planet. Your physical condition will argue against it. Your emotions will cause complications. The good will arise to interfere with the best. Your friends—even Christian ones—will give you reasons not to be serious about it.

On the Thursday before the 1997 Super Bowl, Lora Patterson was rehearsing for the extravaganza's halftime show. Lora, a young woman about to appear on national television, would bungee jump from the top of the New Orleans Superdome. During practice, however, an assistant let out too much line. Lora fell to her death on the Superdome turf. The company in charge of the halftime show recruited inexperienced people and gave them only a two-minute course on managing the bungee cords.

The spiritual correlation is easy to see. Two-minute briefings do not produce maturing Christians. God does not want a church filled with believers who want to enroll in the abbreviated course in discipleship. He telescopes His curriculum for no one. His school is always in session; classes run "day and night."

Remember, many casual Christians in the world (particularly in the United States) will be uncomfortable with the idea that someone they know is getting serious about his or her faith. Your dedication to knowing God through His Word may make them feel uneasy. After all, they may be part of the worldwide school of superficial Christianity.

Removing the Obstacles

Israel was told that it would have to make up its mind: pagan deities or the God of heaven. That same choice still has to be made today.

Sometimes even good things get in the way. On February 27, 1993, after a spring practice outing, Tim Burke walked away from a successful career in professional baseball. The all-star pitcher abandoned the athletic spotlight to spend more time with his wife and their five children—all adopted orphans from other countries. He told a reporter from the *Los Angeles Times:* "Baseball is going to do just fine without me, but I'm the only father my children have." It was a tough choice, but one that earned him respect. He's known in some important circles as the Major League Dad.

The God of the universe waits to be sought, but a million voices clamor for attention and compete with His. What will your choice be?

EXPECTING UPS AND DOWNS

The knowledge of God that is available in this life through meditation is real and valid, but incomplete. What is more, it is fleeting. We do not "arrive" spiritually. We see glimpses, we crest heights, but our knowledge of God is seldom static. Just as David could have his kingdom under control one day and see it crumble around him the next, so we can move from mountain to valley and back again. All this is normal and part of the process of spiritual growth. "The law of the Lord is perfect, reviving the soul" (Psalm 19:7 NIV). There is no point to a statement like that if souls never need reviving.

It ought to go without saying that obedience is critical. The knowledge of God comes through the Word of God, but it also comes through loving the One who gave the Word. We will always be people with unfulfilled longings. But Christians can have those longings dealt with significantly right now, because the Lord has promised to make Himself real to us, if in a limited way: "He who has My commandments and keeps them, it is he who loves Me. And he who loves Me will be loved by My Father, and I will love him and manifest Myself to him" (John 14:21).

Notice that last expression: "I will manifest Myself to Him." Whatever is manifest is open and obvious. How will Jesus Christ make Himself obvious to believers? Two simple conditions: (1) You have to have His commandments, and (2) you have to keep His commandments. Meditation will help you focus on both, and you will find that you know and understand the Lord in a depth you never would have imagined.

There are limitations, of course, to what meditation can do. If we could know Him perfectly now, there would be no reason for His physical presence with us. Yet the Scripture teaches clearly that Jesus Christ will return, bodily and visibly, to set up His kingdom. Our deepest longings will only be satisfied at that time.

Right now, however, we need to recognize that what we really want from life can be found only in the Lord, though He is physically absent. A. W. Tozer once wrote, "If we yearned after God even as much as a cow yearns for her calf, we would be the worshipping and effective believers God wants us to be. If we longed for God as a bride looks forward to the return of her husband, we would be a far greater force for God than we are now."[2]

We look forward to the day when He returns to claim us, so that we may know Him completely. In the interim, we will experience burning hearts when we take up His Word and let it teach us of Him.

MEDITATIONS IN HIS WORD

Realize

Read Psalm 119:17–24.

Reflect

1. In what sort of circumstances might God "hide His commandments" from the psalmist (or us)?

2. Why does he invoke being a "stranger in the earth" as a reason God should not do so?

Respond

1. Are you satisfied with the level of your motivation to know God?

2. Tell Him now how you feel and ask for His mercy and assistance to increase your heart's desire to seek and know Him.

I believe the Bible is the best gift God has ever given to men. All the good from the Savior of the world is communicated to us through this Book.

—Abraham Lincoln

CHAPTER 4

What Meditation Can Do for You

Sometimes we forget that Bible characters felt angry or depressed just like us. Young Timothy, the apostle Paul's quiet friend, was prone to periods of discouragement as he served a church in Ephesus, a city rife with idolatry. Helping his friend, Paul urged Timothy to "exercise" himself toward godliness, which, he insisted, "is profitable for all things, having promise of the life that now is and of that which is to come" (1 Timothy 4:8).

Such godliness issues from thoughtful attention to the Word of God and all its benefits, Paul wrote. "Meditate on these things; give yourself entirely to them. . . Take heed to yourself and to the doctrine" (vv. 15–16). Judging from the apostle's rough treatment as he preached the gospel, it appears that profitability in godliness is not found primarily in what happens to the believer, but in what happens in the believer when obstacles arise. Paul learned to cope with beatings and imprisonments, Timothy with sorrow and timidity.

Wisdom for handling day-to-day events is available too, for you and for me. Not long ago I heard an attractive young Christian businesswoman explain how her faith had proven profitable in solving a recurring problem. Her career duties required a lot of travel.

Asked if she ever experienced problems because of uninvited male attention in airports, she replied, "Not at all. I simply smile sweetly and say five little words, and I am never bothered again."

"And what are the words?" her interviewer asked.

She replied, "I just ask, 'Are you a born-again Christian?'"

Significant benefits await those who take heed to themselves and the doctrines of Scripture. Many of them lie unclaimed, however, because they are available only to those who meditate on the Word of God.

THE BENEFITS OF MEDITATION

The Psalms have more to say about meditation than any book of Scripture. As if to emphasize the value of these jewels of worship and devotion called the Psalms, Psalm 1:1–3 introduces us to the advantages of being a person who meditates:

> Blessed is the man who walks not in the counsel of the ungodly, Nor stands in the path of sinners, nor sits in the seat of the scornful; but his delight is in the law of the Lord, and in His law he meditates day and night. He shall be like a tree planted by the rivers of water, that brings forth its fruit in its season, whose leaf also shall not wither; and whatever he does shall prosper.

Meditation Can Make You Happy

The psalm opens with a description of the one who meditates: "Blessed [happy] is the man who..." People are in desperate pursuit of happiness today. The first psalm tells us where to find it—and it isn't where most people think. People are not happy today because they often have a hazy idea of what constitutes happiness. They think happiness is the set of emotions that exists when their environment is trouble-free. Since no one's environment is ever without its pains, such people are never happy.

Biblically speaking, however, happiness is the settled state of mind that comes from realizing you are the object of divine grace. As such, it lies within the reach of everyone, because it depends not on an external environment but an internal one. Psalm 1 tells us that happiness comes through being the right sort of person, and that comes through meditation on God's Word: "His delight is in the law of the Lord, and in His law he meditates day and night" (v. 2).

Why does meditation produce happiness? Because it makes us realize the greatness of our God and the magnitude of His grace toward us. Genuine happiness comes from knowing Him. God does not usually change our surroundings to make things easier for us. He changes us to make us able to cope with our surroundings. In His original design for humanity, God placed Adam and Eve in an idyllic environment and spent regular time with them. He knew that Paradise was not enough. They needed Him.

Though sin closed Eden, God in His grace granted His Word to the world, and for millennia meditation has been the means by which people have related to Him through that Word. People began meditating as soon as Moses came down from Sinai and began to teach God's people His truth. That truth was taught, digested, memorized, and passed from one household to another for generations (see Deuteronomy 6:6–9). Much of what we know of meditation comes from the pen of David, who meditated on God's truth as he cared for his family's flocks. At the time, only a few books of Scripture had been written, and it could not have been easy for David to discover what they contained. Nonetheless, he read, studied, and memorized what he could, and it made him God's man for a generation.

Meditation Can Make You Wise

In addition to making you happy, meditation can transform you into a wise person. Over time, meditation can enable you to resist the currents of prevailing opinion that tend to distract people from God's purposes. Wisdom is the ability to live life skillfully—which means living that is based on God's truth.[1] Unwholesome influences constitute one of the biggest barriers to doing that. We are not always alert to it, but our minds today are being bombarded with questionable advice. Our friendships can either help us or destroy us.

The person who consistently meditates becomes wise enough to avoid entanglements with people who are likely to have a corrupting effect. The righteous person "walks not in the counsel of the ungodly, nor stands in the path of sinners, nor sits in the seat of the scornful" (v. 1). There is a progression, or rather a retrogression, in this triple description of what the person who meditates refuses to do.

The person who meditates rejects the godless thinking all around him. He "walks not in the counsel of the ungodly." He spurns the counsel of people who want him to be politically correct and morally bankrupt, insisting instead that God's Word will be his standard and focus.

In his wisdom, he will not linger in places frequented by those who reject God's ways. He refuses to "stand in the path of sinners." It is a perilous business to take the advice of the wicked; it is still more dangerous to voluntarily place yourself in a position where their example and advice cannot be avoided. If refusing the counsel of the ungodly describes the righteous person in the realm of *believing,* "not standing in the path of sinners" describes the person who meditates in the realm of *behaving.*

In the conclusion of the triplet in Psalm 1:1, we are told that the person who meditates does not "sit in the seat of the scornful." There the serious believer would find exposure to danger in the realm of *belonging,* for the scornful (or scoffer) is one who not only has rejected the truth for himself, but seeks to entice others to join him. In the human race, it is the scoffer who is furthest from repentance. Getting comfortable with scoffers is the first step to becoming one. Bible commentator Derek Kidner has noted, "The three complete phrases show three aspects, indeed three degrees, of departure from God, by portraying conformity to this world at three different levels: accepting its advice, being party to its ways, and adopting the most fatal of its attitudes."[2]

Meditation Can Make You Stable

Meditation, if practiced faithfully, can also produce in you the stability which is so often commended in Scripture. Our psalm pictures the quality of the person who meditates: "He shall be like a tree planted by the rivers of water" (v. 3). A tree next to an abundant water supply has everything. Its roots are deep and strong, and it becomes a blessing to those near it.

Meditation
Close-up
Meditation: It's Worth It

Reading the Bible only begins the adventure of knowing God; meditation yields even greater benefits. To encourage us to make this practice a part of our lives, the writers of Scripture describe many benefits that come to the believer who meditates:

- Meditation can make you a happy person.
- Meditation can give you God's wisdom.
- Meditation can provide personal stability.
- Meditation can make you productive.
- Meditation can make you a contented person.
- Meditation can make you successful, as God defines success in His Word.

Stability is not deadness, nor should it be confused with inactivity. I read recently the report of a preacher who visited one church. It was "so dead that the termites were holding hands to keep the building from falling down," he wrote.

Bravery and courage form the basis of stability. Being stable means hearing God's voice through the fog of spiritual war. The Duke of Wellington changed the course of European history when his forces defeated Napoleon at Waterloo. He was asked after the battle if his soldiers were braver than those of Napoleon. He said, "No, but they were brave for five minutes longer." That five minutes of stability changed everything.

Stable people don't change the central focus of their lives every few months. They are not inclined to run to the latest seminar or conference simply because it is the hottest thing in Christian circles at the moment. They bloom where God has planted them, and they realize that no job, marriage, or family environment comes without difficulties. Meeting with God in the Word helps make them that way.

Meditation Can Make You Productive

Today his name is a legend, but when he was young, William Carey was known simply as the village cobbler. Soon after his conversion, he began to think about the words of the Lord Jesus: "Go therefore and make disciples of all the nations, baptizing them in the name of the Father and of the Son and of the Holy Spirit, teaching them to observe all things that I have commanded you; and lo, I am with you always, even to the end of the age" (Matthew 28:19–20).

As he meditated, it seemed to William that not many people were leaving England to go to "the nations," and he began to ask impolite questions, such as "Why not?" The answers were unsatisfying, but as one man, what could he do?

Meditation always includes asking oneself, *What does this passage mean to me?* As Carey reflected on the Lord's missionary mandate, he decided that he could at least pray for the nations. So he tacked a map of the world near his workbench as a reminder to pray. As he prayed, he was drawn more and more to the spiritual needs of the world. He began to think of how he might be able to serve God on a foreign field. William figured he would need Bible knowledge and language skills if he could ever get to the mission field, so on his own he mastered Dutch, French, Greek, and Hebrew before he was twenty.

At the age of twenty-two, he joined a local church and soon began preaching on the theme of missions. The results were less spectacular than he had hoped. On one occasion when he was trying to provoke the locals into taking up the cause of reaching the nations, one of the church's leaders admonished him, "Young man, sit down! If God wants to reach the nations with the gospel, He will do it without your help or mine."[3] The church leader did not specify how this would be achieved.

That door being closed, William began looking for a window. He and some like-minded friends formed a missionary society, and eventually William Carey became one of its first missionaries. He settled in India, where he founded a college, began the work of evangelism and church planting, and found the time to translate the Bible into forty-four dialects, making God's Word available to 300 million people. Today he is known as the father of modern missions;

but at one time he was simply a Christian who took a portion of Scripture seriously, and God made him fruitful.

Though less dramatic, meditation can also produce profound changes in the hearts of individuals. It can make you a person who knows his or her priorities and lives them out. It can give you a passion to know God, a tenderness in dealing with people, and a calmness in the face of trials which will astonish your family and friends. That sort of fruitfulness makes a difference. It honors God and attracts people to the Author of the Word.

Meditation Can Make You Contented

"He shall be like a tree . . . that brings forth its fruit in its season" (v. 3). The meditating Christian knows that fruit is seasonal; luscious, tasty fruit does not happen every week or even every three months. As a result, he is satisfied to trust the timing and results of his meditation and his labors to God. He is a contented person. Unfortunately, many people (even Christians, who are supposed to know better) regard contentment as inextricably tied together with possessions.

Some discover the blunder too late. A few years ago a nationally syndicated advice columnist received a story concerning a reader's "Uncle Ollie," a moderately well-to-do miser who distrusted banks. Ollie stashed 20 percent of every paycheck under the mattress in anticipation of a comfortable retirement. When he was sixty, however, Ollie contracted cancer. Shortly before he died, he made his wife promise to place the money he had been saving in his coffin before he was buried so that he could assure himself of entrance into heaven. She quietly agreed. The morning after his death, she deposited the $26,000 in the bank. She then wrote a check for the exact amount and placed it in the casket.

The money in the coffin was a vain attempt to buy contentment. Real contentment comes from knowing God well and recognizing both the vastness of His resources and the enormity of His faithfulness. Such knowledge will come from meditating on the Word regularly.

Meditation Can Make You Successful

"And whatever he does shall prosper" (v. 3). Success is consistently linked with meditation in Scripture. Joshua, confronted with the gargantuan challenge of following in Moses' footsteps, heard directly from God the counsel that would make him a leader: "This Book of the Law shall not depart from your mouth, but you shall meditate in it day and night, that you may observe to do according to all that is written in it. For then you will make your way prosperous, and then you will have good success" (Joshua 1:8). What Joshua needed to do, according to God, was commit himself to a life of meditation. Success would come in due course.

As in fact it did.

After the invitation to meditate, Joshua took thousands of former slaves and invaded a land dotted with fortified cities. At every step, he was resisted by stubborn enemies and difficult friends. Overcoming the people's memories of Moses, Joshua became God's man in his own right. He earned the respect of friend and foe alike, and he set an example of character and persistence that was crucial in the life of the fledgling nation of Israel. And you can bet that, as he was admonished, every day he meditated on the Word of God. It gave him success in the biblical sense.

Money can form part of this kind of success, but meditation's incentive goes deeper than that. The person who meditates prospers at whatever he attempts, because he is inwardly the kind of person whom God takes delight in blessing.

God's Word promises us happiness, stability, productivity, contentment, and success. All we have to do is make it part of us instead of simply part of a Book. Meditation is God's way of doing that.

DOES IT WORK?

The Testimony of Glenn Myers

Glenn Myers is a church consultant who specializes in discipleship and leadership development. In a recent *Discipleship Journal* article, he explained that he is changing into a more joyous person because of his meditation on Scripture.

Several times over the past three years the Lord has brought up the subject of joy through Scriptures I've read and sermons I've heard. I knew that He wanted to produce more of this spiritual fruit in my life. Each time He caught my attention, however, I caved in to busyness. Little fruit resulted.

This time I was determined to heed the Lord's prompting. So over the past several weeks I have focused on joy—memorizing Scriptures on the topic, asking the Lord what has been hindering joy in my life, and writing down what I have been learning. As a result, I'm changing! Much of the heaviness I'd been carrying around due to difficult circumstances has been transformed into praise. Although the problem has not gone away, I am reaping more of the spiritual fruit of joy each day. My wife is finding me much easier to live with![4]

The Testimony of Martin Luther

In a letter to a young colleague, Martin Luther, one of the pivotal figures of church history, gave detailed instructions on how to meditate and the results it would provide. Luther urged, "You should meditate not only in your heart, but also externally, by actually repeating and comparing oral speech and literal words of the book, reading and rereading them with diligent attention and reflection, so you may see what the Holy Spirit means by them."[5]

The one who profits most from the practice will be the one who is persistent, he claimed: "Take care you do not grow weary or think you have done enough when you have read, heard, and spoken them once or twice, and that you then have complete understanding. You'll never be a particularly good theologian if you do that, for you will be like untimely fruit which falls to the ground before it is half ripe."[6]

What happens when meditation is consistently practiced? "If you keep to it, you will become so learned that you yourself could (if it were necessary) write books just as good as those of the fathers and church councils. This is the way taught by holy King David (and doubtlessly used also by all the patriarchs and prophets) in Psalm 119."[7]

The Testimony of Paul Meier

Well-known cofounder of the Minirth-Meier Clinic, Paul Meier says meditation has proved invaluable in his work in helping hurting people. He calls meditation by far the most valuable tool he uses in clinical practice, a counseling tool *par excellence:*

> To prepare myself as a Christian psychiatrist, I undertook college studies, an M.S. degree in human physiology, an M.D. from medical school, psychiatric residency training in two different programs, and theological course work from two evangelical seminaries. During those years I was equipped with many techniques and shortcuts for bringing human beings relief from anxieties, depression, phobias, fears, insecurities, and other kinds of emotional and physical pain. Among the many tools I learned to use, by far the one that has been most valuable in helping people attain spiritual well-being is Scripture meditation.[8]

Meier's research has supported these clinical observations. Some years ago, he supervised a study of personal adjustment among students at a midwestern evangelical seminary. He administered a psychological test, the Minnesota Multiphasic Personality Inventory (MMPI), and an extensive "Spiritual Life Questionnaire." Test results led him to divide participants into three groups: Group A, "those with exceptionally excellent mental health and maturity"; Group B, "those with apparently normal mental health and maturity"; and Group C, "those who were still struggling with statistically significant psychological conflicts and emotional pain."[9]

Meier suspected a strong link between the length of time a student had been a Christian and that student's spiritual and emotional maturity. He then ran statistical analyses in an attempt to correlate the students' mental health with factors on the spiritual life questionnaires. After tabulating the data, he was initially surprised and disappointed. Seminarians who had been Christians for many years did not seem to be significantly better in terms of their mental health than new believers.

Then he noticed a significant pattern:

> I learned one of the most valuable lessons of my life when I found the factor that made the difference. That factor was Scripture meditation. Students who had practiced almost daily Scripture meditation for three years or longer came out, statistically, significantly healthier and happier than students who did not meditate on Scrip-

ture daily. They also came out, statistically, significantly healthier and happier than students who had meditated on Scripture daily for less than three years. The significance level on the various psychological scales varied from the 0.05 level (meaning only one chance in twenty that it was a coincidence) to the 0.001 level (meaning only one chance in a thousand that it was a coincidence).[10]

The Author's Testimony

If Dr. Meier's survey is any indication, meditation is not a quick fix, but it holds out a solid promise of transformation. I found such gradual change to be a reality in my own life. My relationship with my father was terrible until I was well into young adulthood. Like many a dad, he was an expert at finding fault, particularly in his firstborn. I resented for years the way he belittled me and everyone else who was within reach.

During my last year of college, however, my involvement in a campus Christian ministry helped stimulate my interest in the Word of God. To open its pages and drink up the richness of its insights became my greatest delight. Over time, I came to see the folly and sinfulness of my own ways in holding a grudge against my father. Eventually, the Word had its effect, and I was able to forgive him and release the terrible anger I had felt for him for so long. I was even able to share the gospel of the Lord Jesus with him; and though, to my knowledge, he never trusted Christ, I believe he gained a measure of respect for my convictions and for me.

WHY DOES MEDITATION WORK?

How can a relatively simple practice like meditation make such an enormous difference in one's experience? Because it works on a principle that lies at the root of all the dramatic changes God accomplishes: *The Word of God is His chosen instrument of creation and transformation.*

The Word is God's Chosen Instrument of Creation

The writer of Hebrews described how the universe itself came to be: "By faith we understand that the worlds were framed by the word of God, so that the things which are seen were not made of things which are visible" (Hebrews 11:3). When God set out to create the world, He used the most powerful force in existence: His own word. He spoke, and atoms came into existence, combined, and assumed the shapes that He assigned to each.

The psalmist later reflected,

> By the word of the Lord the heavens were made, and all the host of them by the breath of His mouth. He gathers the waters of the sea together as a heap; He lays up the deep in storehouses. Let all the earth fear the Lord; let all the inhabitants of the world stand in awe of Him. For He spoke, and it was done; He commanded, and it stood fast. (Psalm 33:6–9)

If God's Word can accomplish so much, it makes sense to regard Him with awe and adoring fear. If the stupendous accomplishment of the universe itself owes its organization and existence to an utterance breathed out by the Almighty, worship and submission to the Speaker are demanded. What is more, if He chooses to speak at any time—and Christians believe that He has, through His written Word—the product will likewise be creative and powerful.

"By the word of God the heavens were of old," said Peter (2 Peter 3:5). The psalmist, in turn, called on the creation itself to praise God because of His creative Word: "Praise the Lord! Praise the Lord from the heavens. . . . Let them praise the name of the Lord, for *He commanded and they were created*" (Psalm 148:1, 5; italics added).

The Word is God's Chosen Instrument of Transformation

When the time came for the human race to be rescued from its pitiful condition, God's own Son entered human history at a time that fulfilled His Word and was described in terms of His Word: "In the beginning was the Word, and the Word was with God, and the Word was God . . . and *the Word became flesh*" (John 1:1, 14; italics added). The living Word of God became the means by which the world is reconciled to God—the epitome of transformation.

Such transformation comes to all who come under the supernatural authority of the Word. Few more dramatic examples of transforming power exist than an episode from the English revival. George Whitefield was the human instrument at the center of that eighteenth-century awakening. Generally excluded from preaching in churches, he took to open fields and village commons, speaking in his colorful style to crowds often as large as twenty or thirty thousand people. His success in bringing the gospel to English towns and countryside provoked both envy from the clergy and hostility from many others.

One young group of detractors styled themselves the "Hell-Fire Club" and made it their business to ridicule Whitefield by holding their own "gospel meetings." On one occasion, a club member named Thorpe was giving his public imitation of Whitefield, complete with a gospel invitation as he had heard the great evangelist present it. In the middle of his oration Thorpe stopped, pierced to the heart with what he had been saying, and was converted on the spot.[11]

Given the awesome force of God's Word, it ought not to surprise us that He uses it to transform individuals into the image of Christ by giving them renewed minds: "Do not be conformed to this world, but be transformed by the renewing of your mind, that you may prove what is that good and acceptable and perfect will of God" (Romans 12:2). God reveals His will for us in the Word, and that will is that we should all become transformed as we become increasingly like Jesus Christ.

The apostle Paul explicitly links the transformation of Christian wives (through the ministry of their husbands) to the Scriptures: "Husbands, love your wives, just as Christ also loved the church and gave Himself for it, that He might sanctify and cleanse it with the washing of water *by the word,* that He might present it to Himself a glorious church, not having spot or wrinkle or any such thing" (Ephesians 5:25–27, italics added). On the day the Lord Jesus returns, the church will be set apart through the vehicle of God's Word to be everything Jesus Christ wants in a bride.

That transforming power is available to Christian husbands— and to all of us—right now. The sooner we begin to meditate upon it, the sooner things will begin to change in us.

MEDITATIONS IN HIS WORD

Realize

Read Psalm 119:1–8. Notice the use of "blessed" or "happy" in these verses.

Reflect

1. Why do you think Dr. Meier's research was unable to find a link between the amount of time a student had been a Christian and emotional maturity?

2. Why are godly living and joy so closely linked in Scripture? Is there any basis for the popular view that religious people are joyless?

Respond

1. Does joy mark your personal experience? If someone asked a family member or coworker about your countenance, would they describe you as a happy person?

2. Make a list of the fruits of the Spirit that are most prominent in your life. Give God thanks for this evidence of His work.

3. Make a list of the fruits of the Spirit least prominent in your life. Ask God to make these more evident. Using a concordance or topical Bible, make a list of passages related to these qualities.

Go to the ant, you sluggard! Consider her ways and be wise, which, having no captain, overseer or ruler, provides her supplies in the summer, and gathers her food in the harvest.

—King Solomon

CHAPTER 5

The Substance of Meditation

Sir Arthur Conan Doyle's fictional sleuth, Sherlock Holmes, seldom expressed any views on religious subjects. Once, however, while discussing a case with a client, Holmes reflected on the possibility of a good God:

> "What a lovely thing a rose is!"
>
> He [Holmes] walked past the couch to the open window and held up the drooping stalk of a mossrose, looking down at the dainty blend of crimson and green. It was a new phase of his character to me, for I had never before seen him show any keen interest in natural objects.
>
> "There is nothing in which deduction is so necessary as in religion," said he, leaning with his back against the shutters. "It can be built up as an exact science by the reasoner. Our highest assurance of the goodness of Providence seems to me to rest in the flowers. All other things, our powers, our desires, our food, are all really necessary for our existence in the first instance. But this rose is an extra. Its smell and its colour are an embellishment of life, not a condition of it. It is only goodness which gives extras, and so I say again that we have much to hope [for] from the flowers."[1]

Sherlock's observation points us to an important characteristic of meditation. I have been pointing to the text of Scripture as the focus and basic material of meditation. The Word of God sometimes points outside itself, however. God's works form proper subjects for meditation as well as His Word. The Holmesian reverie on the rose is fully in keeping with Scriptural teaching.

THE WORKS OF GOD

What are "the works of God"? They are what God has made or what God has done or both—and the Bible often refers to those works of God. By example and by precept, Scripture points us to such areas. We looked earlier at Psalm 143:5: "I remember the days of old; I meditate on all Your works; I muse on the work of Your hands."

God's works include both the created order ("the work of Your hands"), that is, the so-called natural world, and the events of history. Psalm 102:25 provides an example of the created order: "Of old You laid the foundation of the earth, and the heavens are the work of Your hands."

An example of God's work in history appears in Moses' prayer east of the Jordan as Israel prepared to invade: "O Lord God, You have begun to show Your servant Your greatness and Your mighty hand, for what god is there in heaven or on earth who can do anything like Your works and Your mighty deeds?" (Deuteronomy 3:24). Moses knew God better than anyone alive, and yet was able to see that God had barely displayed the beginnings of His greatness in His works connected with bringing Israel out of Egypt.

An entire theology undergirds Moses' prayer: The events of history are in God's hand. What happens to us for good or ill comes from Him. He has declared Himself vitally interested in everything that touches the believer in Jesus, so He fashions events to suit His purpose (Ephesians 1:11).

God's works are so many and so vast that we will never lack for items to meditate upon. For one thing, we carry untold numbers of them around with us in our own bodies. In *Fearfully and Wonderfully Made*, missionary surgeon Paul Brand described one of God's great works, the design of the DNA molecule:

The secret to membership [in the body] lies locked away inside each cell nucleus, chemically coiled in a strand of DNA. Once the egg and sperm share their inheritance, the DNA chemical ladder splits down the center of every gene much as the teeth of a zipper pull apart. DNA re-forms itself each time the cell divides: 2, 4, 8, 16, 32 cells, each with the identical DNA. Along the ways cells specialize, but each carries the entire instruction book of one hundred thousand genes. DNA is estimated to contain instructions that, if written out, would fill a thousand six-hundred-page books. A nerve cell may operate according to instructions from volume four and a kidney cell from volume twenty-five, but both carry the whole compendium. It provides each cell's sealed credential of membership in the body. Every cell possesses a genetic code so complete that the entire body could be reassembled from information in any one of the body's cells, which forms the basis for speculation about cloning.[2]

Dr. Brand then described the incredible efficiency of the information stored in DNA: "The DNA is so narrow and compacted that all the genes in my body's cells would fit into an ice cube; yet if the DNA were unwound and joined together end to end, the strand could stretch from the earth to the sun and back more than four hundred times."[3]

Solomon commended the natural world as a subject for meditation by pointing the lazy person to the industry of the ant: "Go to the ant, you sluggard! Consider her ways and be wise, which, having no captain, overseer or ruler, provides her supplies in the summer, and gathers her food in the harvest" (Proverbs 6:6–8). Ants don't amount to much in the scheme of things—unless you meditate on them. Consideration of the ant's ways, if taken to heart, can turn the lazy person into a hard worker.

One summer evening several years ago a Christian friend and I sat on his deck marveling at the intricate maneuvers of a spider. We watched the tiny arachnid spin a web, lit from the back by a floodlight, to bridge an unimaginable (from a spider's point of view) chasm. The unsuspecting fly that passed that way had made its last flight, soon finding itself covered from front to back with sticky ropes of spider web. It would be wrong to say that the spider was clever. He was just doing what spiders do.

My friend and I found ourselves appreciative, however, of the engineering skills of the Creator, who took infinite pains with such a tiny part of His creation. God has provided lavishly for spiders. Dare we think He will do less for us?

One of the works of God that has proved most instructive to me is parenthood. Like many fathers, I began my parental experience thinking how fortunate it was for my children that they had me around to teach them what life was all about. Since then, I have been the one getting the education. Today, I thank God for the matchless gift he has given Cheryl and me in the form of our children—and for what meditating on the business of parenting has taught us.

Early in the parenting process, I began to think about my attitude toward my kids. I often found myself in their early years reflecting on two seemingly incompatible facts: (1) how upset I could get with their behavior and (2) how absolutely I loved them. Those times of meditation helped me to understand something of God's own attitudes toward His children. Whenever I have wandered from godly behavior, I have been often comforted by understanding—in some measure—the depth of God's fatherly love, and I have been reproved by knowing that He had a right to expect better of me.

By the way, what part of your kids' behavior makes you the angriest (beside the fact that they remind you so much of yourself, I mean)? I can't speak for everybody, but my children have provoked me most when they have chosen to pay no attention to what I said. Think about that one.

THE WAYS OF GOD

God's works are primarily important because they lead us (or ought to lead us) to a knowledge of God's ways. The two are coupled in the useful statement of Psalm 103:7: "He made known His ways to Moses, His acts to the children of Israel."

The people of Israel saw God's works ("His acts") as He brought them out of Egypt, but they did not recognize how those

Meditation
Close-up
The Works and Wonders of God

Beyond focusing on the Word of God, you and I can meditate on the works of God in order to know God's nature. His works in creation range from the enormous—thundering Niagara Falls and the vast Grand Canyon—to the microscopic—the DNA molecule. Here are some elements of God's creation to meditate on (you may want to do some reading on some of these matters):

- A snowflake
- A child's "baby tooth" placed in a jar
- The industriousness and persistence of the ant
- White blood cells, the body's defense against infection
- The seasons of the year

Besides these wonders of creation, God's works include historical events that show His power and providential care. Here are some points of history to meditate on:

- Jacob and his family, the sons of Israel, are drawn into Egypt by Joseph's presence (and by famine). They become slaves, yet maintain their ethnic and spiritual identity. Eventually the children of Israel become a great nation.
- Jesus feeds a crowd of more than five thousand with only five loaves of bread and two fish. After the meal, His disciples gather twelve baskets of broken leftovers (Matthew 14:15–21).
- Jesus heals the dying son of a royal official instantly after the official pleads for Jesus' help (John 4:46–53).
- In 1947, test pilot Chuck Yeager travels faster than the speed of sound (760 miles per hour), creating a sonic boom. The speed is still only a fraction of the speed of light (186,000 miles per second).
- During the 1990s, scientists continue to discover new stars and galaxies. They predict thousands remain to be discovered in the universe.

works reflected His ways—a far more important bit of knowledge. When I know someone's ways, I can predict (within limits) how he or she might act in a given instance. I understand the person's character. God wants His children to understand Him that way.

The psalmist wrote, "I will meditate on Your precepts, and contemplate Your ways" (Psalm 119:15). "Ways" in a verse like this can mean either "aspects of character" or "teachings"—that is, the ways of God He desires to transmit to us so that our behavior may be godly.

The age to come will be characterized by an increasing knowledge of God's ways: "Many people shall come and say, 'Come, and let us go up to the mountain of the Lord, to the house of the God of Jacob; He will teach us His ways, and we shall walk in His paths.' For out of Zion shall go forth the law, and the word of the Lord from Jerusalem" (Isaiah 2:3).

God's ways are known from Scripture, but also from events as they unfold. David drew an important distinction in Psalm 145:17, "The Lord is righteous in all His ways, gracious in all His works." In other words, His grace, as seen in "His works," is constantly our experience; but whether He treats us apparently well or not, what He does is always right, for all His ways are righteous.

The Christian who meditates will become a careful student of history, biblical and otherwise, for it all lies within God's purview. The believer also will observe his or her own generation and be a student of Scripture. Among those who came to Hebron to acknowledge David's kingship were "the sons of Issachar who had understanding of the times, to know what Israel ought to do" (1 Chronicles 12:32). Understanding the times is part of being a mature believer.

On occasion, we can understand at least part of what God is doing. In the summer of 1967 I played center on the Overseas Crusades (OC) basketball team. Our team toured the Pacific Rim as missionaries. (OC was the pioneer in sports evangelism, dating back to 1952 when they sent their first basketball team to Taiwan.) We played local, regional, or national teams and presented the gospel (usually through translators) at halftime. We ended each halftime talk by offering a free Bible correspondence course.

Our tour included what was then South Vietnam, where we played mostly armed service teams. (The Vietnam War was heating up at that time.) Then we boarded the airplane for our next stop: Hong Kong.

After only a half hour of flying, however, the pilot informed us that we were turning back to Saigon due to mechanical trouble. We were to be kept overnight and catch the same flight out the next day.

That evening, exhausted from dragging our suitcases and equipment up eleven flights of stairs (there was no elevator in the hotel), we gathered for prayer, wondering aloud what God's purpose might be in delaying our trip. The next day my teammate George Terzian found himself sitting on the plane next to a distinguished-looking gentleman of Chinese extraction, the employee of a Taiwanese company. He had been engaged in construction work for the U.S. military command in Saigon and was on his way home to Taipei for a long-overdue vacation and to see his family.

George began to inquire into his spiritual condition, but the man soon stopped him. "I know where you're headed," he said. "My wife is a third-generation Christian. She has been praying for me for thirty years and has told me about Christ many times. I'm just not interested."

Even though George respected his stated desire to be spared hearing the gospel again, as the plane neared its destination, Hong Kong, the man returned to the subject himself. In a few minutes, George went through the truth of the gospel with him in a personal way. By the time the flight landed, a new name had been added to God's citizenship roll in heaven. Our team gathered that afternoon with great joy, privileged to at least have an idea why God had blue-penciled our schedule.

TRYING TO UNDERSTAND GOD'S WAYS

We meditate on His ways, yet all the while acknowledging that God's characteristics are ultimately unsearchable. He may be totally faithful, but unless He has told us His plans in Scripture, He is not totally predictable: "When I applied my heart to know wisdom and to see the business that is done on earth . . . I saw all the work of

God, that a man cannot find out the work that is done under the sun. For though a man labors to discover it, yet he will not find it; moreover, though a wise man attempts to know it, he will not be able to find it" (Ecclesiastes 8:16–17).

Unfortunately, Christians often suffer when they presume they know the big picture. Take the incident involving Roger Simms. He would never forget the day he was discharged from the Army, May 7. He was ready to become a civilian again, but first he needed a ride home. Holding out his thumb toward the passing traffic, he was surprised to find a new Cadillac had stopped for him. [4]

The passenger door opened invitingly. Roger quickly tossed his luggage in the back and thanked the driver, an obviously successful businessman, who asked, "Going home for keeps?"

"Sure am," Roger responded.

"Well, you're in luck if you're going to Chicago."

"Not quite that far. Do you live in Chicago?"

"I have a business there. My name is Hanover."

After the small talk had slowed down, Roger, a Christian, wondered whether he should attempt to share the gospel with his benefactor. When he realized that his hometown was only minutes away, he decided to speak: "Mr. Hanover, I would like to talk to you about something important."

Roger then explained the way of salvation and ended by asking Mr. Hanover if he would like to receive Christ. Suddenly the Cadillac pulled over to the side of the road. Roger wondered if he was about to have to walk the rest of the way home, but the businessman had something else on his mind. He quite eagerly expressed a desire to know Christ, and at Roger's suggestion humbly bowed his head and invited the Lord to take up residence within him and grant him eternal life. With tears in his eyes, he turned to Roger, saying, "This is the greatest thing that has ever happened to me."

Five years later, Roger was married and both a father and businessman. While packing his suitcase for a business trip to Chicago, he came across the business card Mr. Hanover had given him on that day he was discharged. He decided to look in on Mr. Hanover's business to see how he was. In Chicago, the company receptionist explained that Mr. Hanover was unavailable, but that he could see Mrs. Hanover. She stood up to meet him with outstretched hand: "You knew my husband?"

Roger, somewhat chilled by the use of the past tense, recounted the events on his ride home.

"Can you tell me when that was?"

"It was May 7, five years ago, the day I was discharged from the army."

"Anything special about that day?"

Roger hesitated. Should he mention her husband's profession of faith? He decided to go ahead. "Mrs. Hanover, I explained the gospel of Christ to him. He pulled over to the side of the road and wept against the steering wheel. He put his trust in Christ that day."

Mrs. Hanover burst into tears. After calming herself, she explained, "I prayed for my husband's salvation for years. I believed God would save him."

Roger asked, "And where is your husband, Mrs. Hanover?"

"He's dead," she explained. "He was in a car crash after he let you out of the car. He never got home. You see . . . I stopped living for God five years ago because I thought God had not kept His word!"

Many of us, when we pray, are secretly asking for two favors. We want God to answer our prayers, and we want Him to show us that He has answered our prayers. We not only want people converted, we want to know that they are converted. Our knowledge of God's ways will always be limited; it makes sense to trust Him for what we can't know.

THE WORD OF GOD

When it comes to assessing whether objects or events are displaying God's ways or obscuring, let us not forget that the controlling source is always to be the Scriptures. The works of God and the ways of God are always best understood with the revealing backlight of the Word of God. That backlight gives truth, for the Scriptures are inerrant.

God does place one condition on success in meditation, however: The believer must not mock Him through indifference to those truths he discovers in the Word. Relating to God's truth is not like learning mathematics. We are supposed to be motivated by more than curiosity. Obedience is the fundamental response He expects. We think deeply on His Word because it is His Word. Beyond meditating upon the sacred page, we seek to know its Author.

MEDITATIONS IN HIS WORD

Realize

Read Matthew 6:25–34.

Reflect

1. The Lord Jesus insisted that ample evidence of God's faithfulness lies all around us. What two examples does He use in this passage to prove His point? What particular need does each example address?

2. What is the central command of this passage of Scripture?

3. The Lord rarely made direct criticisms of His disciples as He did here. What aspect of their spiritual lives did He find fault with? Is this related to the central command discussed above? How?

4. This same criticism occurs in other portions of the gospel accounts. Use your concordance to discover them. What do they have in common with this section? In what ways do they differ?

Respond

1. List any areas where you are failing to trust God. Confess your lack of faith to God (1 John 1:9).

2. Does worry plague your life? Ask God to help you get this part of your experience under control.

Although you may have no commentaries at hand, continue to read the Word and pray; for a little from God is better than a great deal received from a man. Too many are content to listen to what comes from men's mouths, without searching and kneeling before God to know the real truth. That which we receive directly from the Lord through the study of His Word is from the minting house itself. Even old truths are new if they come to us with the smell of heaven upon them.

—John Bunyan

CHAPTER 6

Seeking God's Truth in the Word

Several years ago a family from our congregation (I will call them the Johnsons) moved to a small town in west Georgia and soon afterward began looking for a new church home. One assembly was especially near their new residence, so John and Joanne attended there first. On the occasion of their initial visit, after hymns had been sung and prayer had been offered, the time came when someone usually begins to expound the Scriptures. However, in this church, nothing happened. The man who was apparently to be the speaker sat at the front, but he did not rise to say anything. Time passed in silence. The Johnsons were beginning to get a little uncomfortable when finally the speaker rose and began to address the group.

After the service they discovered that the speaker, who was the church's pastor, made it his practice never to prepare a sermon, but simply to come to church and wait for God to "speak" to him. On some occasions, God apparently had nothing to say, and people went home with no word from the Lord. The Johnsons decided to look elsewhere for a church home.

It never ceases to amaze me how professing Christians—and

even church leaders like that pastor—can be so indifferent to the Scriptures. God has gone to enormous lengths to preserve His Word for us and transmit it to us; yet many Christians are not satisfied with that. Often we want it customized for us as individuals and transmitted to us via direct revelation. We can't be troubled to search the Bible, to think deeply about its contents. Meanwhile, some teachers and preachers are not willing to prepare a message for their people based on its teaching.

There may be many reasons for this casual attitude, but I am convinced that in a few cases the true explanation is arrogance. Some Christians feel that while it is acceptable for God to provide the Bible for most, they are deserving of a personalized revelation from God.

Such expectations sometimes produce odd results. A friend once told me about a classmate at a small Christian college who wanted to hear directly from God. The student, whom I'll call Jeff, was unpopular at the school because he loved to parade his spirituality. Jeff was inclined to pray aloud late at night in his dorm room, going on and on in a voice that was almost a shout. The young men on the floor above him would be about to fall asleep when the prayer exhibition would jar them from their drowsiness.

Jeff felt he was a person of destiny, with great things ahead of him. In his loud nocturnal devotions, he would pray, "Lord, where do You want me to go? What do You want me to do?" as though he expected a direct and immediate answer instead of using the Word and sound wisdom to draw godly conclusions. The guys in the room above heard this prayer so often during the school year that they finally decided to do something about it.

Now they should have just taken him aside and asked him to do his praying more quietly or at a reasonable hour, but that is not always the way of young men. One of the guys owned a sophisticated stereo system with a public address capability. One fateful night he inserted a microphone into his stereo, lowered a speaker out his window so that it hung just above the window of the loud pray-er's room, and sat down to wait for the pleas to come. Sure enough, about the expected time came the famous question: "Lord, where do You want me to go?"

Suddenly Jeff heard, "Go to Switzerland" in a deep and dignified tone. Of course, he did a double take. But since the answer had been provided, the next question was in order: "What do You want me to do?"

Again the answer: "Convert the Swiss."

To this day the man lives in Switzerland as a self-appointed missionary. Nobody thought enough of him to tell him that it was all a practical joke. Though I applaud the young man's desire to do God's will, I wish he had based his commitment on the firm ground of biblical revelation instead of listening to dubious voices in the night.

Actually, the modern taste for customized revelation goes back centuries. Even Martin Luther, that giant of the Reformation, was briefly caught in the same trap. For a while, when he was scheduled to speak in church he would sit and wait for God to "speak" to him. One day that all changed. According to Luther, God indeed spoke to him, and this was His message: "Martin, you're unprepared."[1]

After that, he had something to say before he went into the pulpit.

A lot of Christians face life unprepared. They go out to face the day without meeting with the Lord in the Word. Many an excuse is trotted out in an effort to justify this dubious omission. Perhaps none is as often used or as invalid as the idea that the Bible is just too obscure for the ordinary Christian to understand.

This excuse is suspect. Consider that some of the Bible's most distinguished interpreters and writers were shepherds and fishermen. Even a superficial examination reveals that the Bible was written for the ordinary person, and its truths are accessible to everyone. Anyone who can read a newspaper with comprehension can read the Bible with comprehension. Anyone who can read an ordinary letter can study with profit God's awesome Word.

Providing a complete course in Bible reading and study methods is beyond the scope of this book. What follows is a summary of some of the basics. As you read, please remember that the attitude you bring to the Bible is much more important than the mechanics of how you study. Read the Scriptures as God's love letter to you (which it is), and you will find more than enough spiritual food.

READING THE WORD

Extensive Reading

Extensive reading of Scripture—covering the Bible once a year, for example—isn't nearly as challenging as people sometimes think. Reading the Bible at "pulpit speed," a thoughtful, moderate pace for comprehension, requires about seventy-eight hours. Divide that figure by 365, and you discover that the Bible can be read each year in its entirety with an investment of about twelve minutes per day—hardly a heroic effort. Many publishers have facilitated the process by placing daily reading schedules in the end papers of their Bibles.

Such an extensive reading approach will keep us from ignoring significant areas of truth to which we need periodic reexposure. When I was a seminary student, the beloved Dr. J. Vernon McGee served as one of our special Bible lecturers. I remember his advising us during a question and answer time, "Men, preach through the Bible—it will keep you from riding your hobby horse." The same principle applies to reading through the Bible. *All* Scripture is inspired and profitable—and ought to be read.

Larger portions are difficult to use in meditation, however, which must necessarily major on smaller and more manageable sections.

Intensive Reading

The meditative process begins with a reading of the text. This should be done in a Bible translation, not a paraphrase, and preferably not a study Bible. (There is a place for paraphrases and study Bibles, but not here. You want to perceive the truth with "the smell of heaven" upon it, to use Bunyan's expressive phrase.)

Reading should be done in the same version most of the time. Irving Jensen, late professor of Bible at Bryan College and author of dozens of books on Bible study, insisted that Bible reading accomplishes the most when certain practices are observed.[2] Jensen taught that believers should read carefully, repeatedly, aloud, at different speeds, and with tools in hand.

Read carefully. Everyone has lifted his eyes from a page of text and realized that the words he just "read" had been passed over without being absorbed. God went to a great deal of trouble to provide us with the Word; He deserves to have it taken seriously. Read as though your life depends on it. It does (Deuteronomy 32:47)!

Read repeatedly. I played basketball in college under legendary coach John Wooden, a man noted for his aphorisms. Coach Wooden often said about our UCLA teams, "We don't shoot particularly well, but we do shoot often." You will not always score (that is, receive an insight or application) while reading a passage the first time. Shoot again; there are points to be made. G. Campbell Morgan used to read a passage fifty to a hundred times before preaching or writing on it. His books are still in print decades after his death. There's a connection.

Read aloud. People are often surprised to discover that silent reading is a relatively recent invention. For centuries apparently no one thought of doing it that way. You may remember the Ethiopian who was on his way home from a festival in Jerusalem. Dr. Luke records, "So Philip ran to him, and *heard him reading* the prophet Isaiah, and said, 'Do you understand what you are reading?'" (Acts 8:30, italics added). The Ethiopian was reading aloud while sitting in his chariot.

Reading aloud involves not only our minds but also our hearing. As a result of the dual exposure, surprising insights may be discovered. Nuances and connections are grasped that are commonly missed while reading silently.

Read at different speeds. Read at a rapid pace to get the overall idea and theme in mind. Every passage, like every day, has a context that informs and helps make sense of it. Spending a few seconds reading the paragraphs before and after the target text will yield disproportionately large results.

Read at a moderate rate when first confronting the target text. Survey the text for its larger ideas; note especially the beginning and ending of your study portion and how they relate to one another and the context.

Finally, read slowly and thoughtfully when you begin to do your serious thought work. Remember George Washington Carver's dictum: "Anything will give up its secrets if you love it enough."

Read with tools in hand. A pencil is useful for jotting down quick observations or questions in the margin. At this point, you are not necessarily attempting to solve problems or answer questions; but your reading ought to surface them. A pad of paper will be helpful for making notes that are too large for your Bible's margins.

What—notes in the margins? Mark up my Bible? Absolutely. Mark it up. Dog-ear it. Highlight it. Draw arrows and circles. Underline to your heart's content. Your Bible will need to be replaced sooner (I go through a Bible about every two or three years), but you will be the better for it. As it has often been said, "A Bible that is falling apart usually belongs to someone who isn't." Naturally, you will want to avoid doing your reading and study in the "family Bible." That one is reserved for pressing flowers and preserving letters and locks of hair. You can find an inexpensive paper or cloth-backed Bible for study at your local Christian bookstore.

STUDYING THE WORD

Productive Bible study normally involves a three-step process: (1) observe the text, (2) interpret the text, and (3) apply the text. First, look carefully to see what is there, and then draw the meaning from what you see. Finally, on the basis of that meaning, let the Word change the way you behave and think.

Observe: What Do I See?

Howard Hendricks, long-time professor at Dallas Theological Seminary, taught two generations of ministers how to study the Bible. He suggests that observation be done with an eye toward five realities.[3] While studying a Scripture passage, we are to look at things that are (1) emphasized, (2) repeated, (3) related, (4) alike or unalike, and (5) true to life.

Things that are emphasized. Hendricks first recommends we observe the passage's emphasis. Why such emphasis on emphasis? The writers of Scripture, superintended by the Holy Spirit, communicated their intent often by (1) the amount of space they devoted to an issue, or (2) by the order in which items are presented, or (3) by overt statements of purpose.

An example of the first may be seen in the gospels written by

Mark and Matthew. Mark emphasized the actions—especially the miracles—of Jesus and omitted much of His teaching ministry. His account intended to show the power and prerogatives of the Lord Jesus. Matthew, by contrast, devoted about a third of his account to the major discourses of the Lord. In one gospel, brief teachings framed narratives of mighty acts. In the other, events set the stage for the teachings.

An example of the second kind of emphasis, the order of presentation, may be seen in the familiar pattern of Paul's writings. His letters nearly always begin with a section of doctrine (Ephesians 1–3; Colossians 1–2), followed by a portion in which the doctrine is applied to behavior (Ephesians 4–6; Colossians 3–4). In Paul's thinking, knowing the truth is always the basis for living it.

An example of the third sort of emphasis, overt purpose statements, occurs in John 20:30–31, "Truly Jesus did many other signs in the presence of His disciples, which are not written in this book; but these are written that you may believe that Jesus is the Christ, the Son of God, and that believing you may have life in His name." John is the one gospel written with unbelievers in mind, and with the intention of making believers of them. It is the greatest gospel tract ever written, to say nothing of its peerless glorification of Jesus Christ.

Luke's rather different purpose appears at the beginning of his gospel: "Inasmuch as many have taken in hand to set in order a narrative of those things which have been fulfilled among us . . . it seemed good to me also, having had perfect understanding of all things from the very first, to write to you an orderly account, most excellent Theophilus, that you may know the certainty of those things in which you were instructed" (Luke 1:1, 3–4). This is a direct and definite purpose statement. Luke, a physician, wrote to a man who was apparently (from the term used in addressing him) a Roman official and probably a believer, since he had received instruction in the faith. Luke wrote in order to establish the exact truth of the events of the life of Christ. Luke understood that Christian faith is based on the facts of history rather than wishful thinking. It does make a difference that Jesus Christ came out of that tomb in Jerusalem. Personal certainty is based on historical certainty. Thus his accounts of the gospel in Luke and in Acts focus on events, on the historical record.

Things that are repeated. Meditation involves keeping an eye peeled for the repetition of key words or phrases. The author uses such clues to keep us pointed in the direction of his thought. For example, the little words *all* and *none* form the heart of what Paul is teaching in Romans 3:9–12:

> We have previously charged both Jews and Greeks that they are all under sin. As it is written: "There is none righteous, no, not one; there is none who understands; there is none who seeks after God. They have all gone out of the way; they have together become unprofitable; there is none who does good, no, not one."

A universal need demands a universal salvation, as the apostle subsequently explains. No one is exempt from this need. Not one. The repetition of terms helps us see the direction of the apostolic argument.

Things that are related. Questions and answers, cause and effect, negatives and positives—all these help the writers of Scripture convey their purpose. When Paul asked, "What shall we say then? Shall we continue in sin that grace may abound?" (Romans 6:1), we know two things: (1) someone was suggesting that Christians should sin for just that purpose, and (2) Paul was about to answer the question he has just posed—in the negative, of course.

Describing the latter days of Solomon's rule, God's Word says that "King Solomon loved many foreign women . . . from the nations of whom the Lord had said to the children of Israel, 'You shall not intermarry with them'" (1 Kings 11:1–2). In the middle of the same chapter, the comment is made twice that the Lord "raised up an adversary against Solomon" (1 Kings 11:14, 23). The adversaries were the effects of which Solomon's disobedience was the cause.

Things that are alike or unalike. Figures of speech, such as similes and metaphors, provide fertile ground for meditation. Similes are indirect comparisons, such as, "He's busy as a beaver"; metaphors are direct comparisons, such as, "Cheryl is a cuddly teddy bear, soft, soothing, and always at my side." In the Scriptures, such images are significant. When God is described as "my Rock" (Psalm

28:1; 31:2) or the "Shepherd of Israel" (Psalm 80: 1), the figure ought to be noted for later reflection and exploration.

Conjunctions and adverbs often provide clues to where a passage is headed. Words like "but," "nevertheless," and "although" often give away the author's intent. The Bible student must always ask what the "therefore" is there for.

Things that are true to life. The Bible is a realistic book. Its heroes have clay feet, and some of its villains exhibit redeeming qualities. Taking stock of the bad examples as well as the good is part of observation.

Samuel is rightly considered one of the godliest men in all of Scripture. He proved to be a rock of integrity in dealing with Saul and his failures as the leader of God's people. However, as a father his own deficiencies were many and obvious. The leaders of Israel eventually called him to account over it:

> When Samuel was old he made his sons judges over Israel. But his sons did not walk in his ways; they turned aside after dishonest gain, took bribes, and perverted justice. Then all the elders of Israel gathered together and came to Samuel at Ramah, and said to him, "Look, you are old, and your sons do not walk in your ways. Now make us a king to judge us like all the nations." (1 Samuel 8:1, 3–5)

Can a man do well in ministry and fail miserably in his home? That outcome is all too common, I fear. Such realities are there in the text for all who are alert to them.

Interpret: What Does It Mean?

Next in the study process comes interpreting the facts you have observed. Often this process is so simple that it requires no more expertise than the kind you use in reading the minutes of the PTA meeting. Our minds work so rapidly that we can often form a correct interpretation of a verse by the time we finish reading it. However, when difficulties do arise, proper interpretation must be done, giving due respect to the following areas: (1) content, (2) context, (3) comparison, (4) culture, and (5) consultation.[4]

Content. The intent of Scripture is conveyed the same way meaning is conveyed in the morning newspaper: by the content of

ferent, settled environment in which their biblical heritage shaped public and private life. Then consider the apostle Paul, an urban man who was multilingual. He lived in a world dominated by Greco-Roman culture.

Today, however, the culture of the Bible—whatever it is—is routinely used as a reason to dismiss its teachings as outmoded. It's a cheap way of avoiding biblical teachings and implications: "It's old; throw it out." A proper respect for culture in interpretation actually means, however, that you attempt to gain enough knowledge of the culture to understand the meaning of a passage when the two are connected. New Testament writers such as Paul never used cultural differences to dismiss the teachings of their own Bible (what we call the Old Testament).

The apostle did not live in Abraham's or Moses' time, and he probably never lived on a farm; but he knew enough agriculture to realize what oxen did there. Even more importantly, he understood that when God warned Israel not to muzzle the ox as it treaded out the grain (Deuteronomy 25:4), He had more in mind than oxen. So Paul wrote the Corinthians:

> It is written in the law of Moses, "You shall not muzzle an ox while it treads out the grain" [Deuteronomy 25:4]. Is it oxen God is concerned about? Or does He say it altogether for our sakes? For our sakes, no doubt, this is written, that he who plows should plow in hope, and he who threshes in hope should be partaker of his hope. (1 Corinthians 9:9–10)

What appears to be an obscure text about not muzzling an ox forms the heart of Paul's argument about the propriety of being financially supported as a minister of the gospel. God's way from the earliest times, says the apostle, is to allow those who labor to share in the fruits of that labor.

Paul understood that the Bible spans many cultures, but so do its teachings. They are not relevant only to some bygone culture. The teachings remain timely, because they are timeless. Cultures change; people don't.

Consultation. The wise student will make good use—but not overuse—of Bible study tools. I have often told people that if I were shipwrecked on some desert isle I would hope that the island bookstore would have a copy of *Strong's Concordance;* after the Bible itself, *Strong's* would become my most prized possession. A concordance lets me find any verse as well as see how a key term is used in other Bible verses (and it often includes root meanings of the word). A good Bible dictionary would be helpful too—preferably one compiled within the last twenty years or so and the product of an evangelical publishing house.

Commentaries by the experts (theologians and Bible scholars) help you understand the content and meaning of specific Bible books. A word of caution, however. Avoid spending a lot of time in commentaries. Don't get me wrong; Bible commentaries have their place. If I could get retail price for the commentaries in my own library, I could probably buy a new car. They do suffer from two major drawbacks, however. First, they tend to shortcut meditation and the joys of discovery by providing answers before the questions are asked. As a result, they often become a crutch, particularly for young Christians. The second problem is that they often ignore the exact question for which you want an answer. In fact, McIntosh's First Law of Commentaries is: The likelihood of a specific interpretive issue being addressed by a commentary is inversely proportional to the intensity of my interest in the issue.

The time to consult commentaries is after you have done your personal study. You may find by reading a commentary that you have overlooked some significant difficulty, or that there are resolutions to problems in the text which you had not considered in your personal study.

One interpretation: the principle of analogy. Remember as you study that a passage of Scripture has only one meaning. The one valid meaning of the morning newspaper, or that letter from your mother, or the text of the Bible is *that which the author(s) intended.* We are not free to inject views of reality onto the page which God and the human author of the text did not intend. This meaning is the interpretation of the passage. There is only one interpretation.

However, there may be many valid applications of a text. We apply the Bible to ourselves on the principle of analogy. That is, we take the similarities between ourselves and the original readers and apply the meaning of the text on the basis of those similarities. Paul told the Thessalonian believers, "Rejoice always" (1 Thessalonians 5:16). What is the intent of the text? That the Thessalonian believers should rejoice constantly. However, since the Thessalonian believers are typical in most respects, and since the same sentiment appears elsewhere in Scripture, it is perfectly valid to *apply* the text to Christians across the board.

Apply: What Does It Mean to Me?

An excellent way to apply the text of Scripture is to conceive of yourself at the center of a series of concentric circles. You apply the text from the inside out, always beginning with your own heart. (Application may logically belong in the "reflection" stage of meditation. I am including it here for simplicity's sake.)

Personal life. Ask yourself, "Does this text give me a command to obey? An example to follow? A sin to forsake? Does it rebuke an attitude or habit pattern that I need to change?" This is the most important circle. Here is where values are formed. Whatever happens in the meditation process at this level will affect everything else.

Family life. Meditating means asking, "Does this passage touch on my relationship to my mate? To my children? To my parents? To my siblings? How can I avoid the Samuel syndrome—having public success and a family disaster?"

Church life. Next comes the spiritual family. Ask yourself: "What does the passage teach or imply about my involvement in my local church? Does it suggest a needed ministry in which I may get involved? Does it argue for an increased involvement in an existing ministry? Are there suggestions in it that my prayer life should be refocused to support the church's ministries in a new way?"

Work. Application requires asking, "Does the text speak to my occupation directly? Indirectly? Is my faith working at work? Do people at work respect me? Are my work habits an adornment or a reproach of the doctrines I profess?"

Community and world. The outer circle demands that I ask myself, "Does the passage suggest a way in which I might be a blessing in my neighborhood? In my city? How does this text touch on my involvement in world missions?"

To reiterate: Don't let the mechanics of Bible study get in your way. These guidelines are just that. If you treasure God's Word, you will find a way to uncover its wonders, particularly if you make a passage like Psalm 86:11 your personal prayer: "Teach me Your way, O Lord; I will walk in Your truth; unite my heart to fear Your name." Prayer for wisdom is always the reasonable prelude to a time of study.

MEDITATIONS IN HIS WORD

Realize

Read Jonah 4:1–11.

Reflect

1. This is a remarkable account for many reasons. For one, it displays disappointing behavior on Jonah's part right to the very end. For another, his anger seems misdirected. What exactly is Jonah's complaint about God (v. 2)?

2. Who probably wrote this book? Do you see anything hopeful in that?

3. God resolved His relationship with the Ninevites more easily than His relations with His erring prophet. What attitude does God exhibit in His conversations with Jonah?

Respond

1. Do you possess any attitude kinship with Jonah? You might want to pray something like David's prayer: "Search me, O God, and know my heart; try me, and know my anxieties; and see if there is any wicked way in me, and lead me in the way everlasting" (Psalm 139:23–24).

Your word I have hidden in my heart, that I might not sin against You.

—King David

CHAPTER 7

Retaining God's Truth

E. Schuyler English, a Bible teacher and coeditor of the *New Scofield Reference Bible,* often related to his conference audiences how God had touched a small village in eastern Poland. During the 1930s, Michael Billester, an itinerant bookseller, had visited a poor hamlet in that region and, finding no one able to afford a Bible, had given one to a villager. The recipient read it, was converted, and began to share his Bible with others in the village.

Slowly but surely other people came to know Christ through that Bible and the testimony of their newly converted neighbors. Eventually some two hundred people—practically the entire community—became Christian believers.

When Billester returned to the village in 1940, he was delighted to see what had happened, and the townspeople were equally glad to see him. Since the Lord's Day was close at hand, the villagers asked him to speak during the service. At the appointed time, Billester suggested that instead of giving testimonies members of the church should recite verses of Scripture.

At this point, a man stood and asked, "Perhaps we misunderstood. Did you mean verses or chapters?"

"Do you mean to say that there are people here who can recite chapters of the Bible?" asked Mr. Billester in astonishment.

That was exactly what he meant.

Those humble villagers had memorized not only chapters, but whole books of Scripture. Some knew Matthew and Luke and half of Genesis. One man had committed the Psalms to memory. Together, the two hundred people had memorized nearly the entire Bible. Billester's old gift Book had become so worn with the years that its pages were barely legible, but it had found a home where it could remain and endure.

WHAT? ME MEMORIZE?

Now before you toss this book into the "never to be picked up again" pile, let me assure you that I will not ask you to duplicate the memory feats of those dear Polish villagers. I tell the story because they were people who could never be accused of possessing special advantages when it came to memorizing Scripture. I doubt that many of them would have fit into the category we call "brilliant." They owned only one copy of the Bible to share among two hundred people.

They would not have considered what they did a "feat of memory" at all. They were merely people who saw what was supremely valuable and went after it. If everyone had owned a copy of the Bible, they might not have memorized as much as they did. The convenience of having a Bible at their fingertips might have lulled them, as it does us, into complacency.

The primary motivation for memorizing Scripture, however, is not the threat of losing our printed copies. It is the importance of being on close terms with its content and with its Author. And there is another reason. The phrase "day and night" commonly appears in Scripture in connection with meditation. If I can't have my Bible open and in front of me all day—and for most people that is neither possible nor practical—then intermittent meditation will have to be done on the strength of the Scriptures I can remember. Memory work is a practical necessity for a person who wants to meditate "day and night."

People sometimes struggle in coming to grips with what is

truly important in life. Perversely, we seem to recognize it only when it is missing. Take the case of Howard Rutledge, who was a prisoner of war (POW) in Vietnam for seven years. While incarcerated at the prison the Americans called Heartbreak Hotel in Hanoi, he discovered an aching absence in his life.

> During those longer periods of enforced reflection it became so much easier to separate the important from the trivial, the worthwhile from the waste. For example, in the past, I usually worked or played hard on Sundays and had no time for church. For years Phyllis had encouraged me to join the family at church. She never nagged or scolded—she just kept hoping. But I was . . . too preoccupied to spend one or two short hours a week thinking about the really important things.
>
> Now the sights and smells of death were all around me. My hunger for spiritual food soon outdid my hunger for a steak. Now I wanted to know about that part of me that will never die. Now I wanted to talk about God and Christ and the church. But in Heartbreak solitary confinement, there was no pastor, no Sunday School teacher, no Bible, no hymnbook, no community of believers to guide and sustain me. I had completely neglected the spiritual dimension of my life. It took prison to show me how empty life is without God.[1]

Several of the camp inmates tell in their memoirs how the POWs began to share Scripture verses they had memorized. They would tap on the walls between their cells in a special code, pecking out the words of verses that they had remembered. The Word of God became incredibly precious to them. They became imitators of Job, who said, "I have not departed from the commandment of His lips; I have treasured the words of His mouth more than my necessary food" (Job 23:12).

Given its value during the difficult times, why is memorization of Scripture such an uncommon practice among those of us who are free to do so? I fear that many of us stay away from memorizing because of the way it is presented to us. Let me explain.

TWO APPROACHES TO MEMORIZING

The Storehouse Approach

The approach to memory work that most of us are familiar with I am choosing to call *the storehouse approach*. As the name implies, this method hands us a list of cards with references on one side and complete verses on the other and says: "Memorize these. You might need them some day."

There is nothing intrinsically wrong with this method. I have used it myself with profit. I would never try to argue someone out of doing memory work using the storehouse approach. It may be the best method to help children and young people memorize Scripture—especially since they are at an age when their memorizing ability far exceeds their judgment. They benefit from key verses, already chosen, that can inform, encourage, inspire, and warn. And our youth can memorize well:

> Youth has been called the golden age of memory. Nell Fichthorn, Director of Music at Sandy Cove Bible Conference, Maryland, counted fifty-five songs his youth choir learned in the first two months of the 1983 summer conference, an average of almost one a day. These complete songs, usually with several verses, were well remembered weeks after originally learned.[2]

The storehouse approach to memory work has its place. But there is an alternative.

The Workshop Approach

The workshop approach to memorization does not pay special attention to whether the one memorizing will be able to repeat the text perfectly five years from today. Workshop memorization focuses on the short term, enabling the one meditating to recall and mull over the text at the place he is working in Scripture. Using this approach, if I memorize a verse each week, I may or may not be able to repeat it exactly three years from now. Yet if I can learn it well enough to use it for a couple of weeks, that is enough.

Because "the word of God is living and powerful, and sharper than any two-edged sword, piercing even to the division of soul and

Meditation
Close-up
Passages Addressing Personal Issues

Here are twenty-eight topics, all useful for Scripture memorization. (See discussion under "What to Memorize" and "How to Memorize" for tips and ideas on Scripture memorizing.) The act of memorizing will help you meditate on God's perspective on these personal issues.

Anger	Proverbs 14:17, 29; 15:1; James 1:19–20; Ephesians 4:25–32
Assurance	Romans 3:21–26; 5:1–5; 1 John 5:13, 18, 19
Complaining	James 5:7–12
Contentment	Psalm 37; Philippians 4:10–13; Hebrews 13:5
Courage	Psalm 27; Proverbs 28:1; 2 Timothy 1:7
Depression	Genesis 4:6–7; Psalms 32, 38, 51; 2 Corinthians 4:8–9
Doubt	Psalm 42:5; John 20:25, 27; Isaiah 49:14–15
Drunkenness	Proverbs 23:29–35; 31:4–6
Envy	James 3:13–18
Fear	Matthew 10:26–31; 1 Peter 3:6, 13–14; 1 John 4:18
Forgiveness	Psalm 32; Matthew 18:15–17; Luke 17:3–10
Greed	1 Timothy 6:17–19
Grief	1 Thessalonians 4:13–18
Honesty	Deuteronomy 25:13–16; 1 Thessalonians 4:11–12
Humility	Philippians 2:1–11
Joy	Psalm 34; Philippians 4:4–9
Laziness	Proverbs 26:13–16
Pride	1 Peter 5:5–11
Resentment	Proverbs 26:24–26
Sexual Sin	1 Corinthians 5:1–13; 6:18–20; 1 Thessalonians 4:1–8
Steadfastness	2 Timothy 3:10–17; 2 Peter 3:14–18
Suffering	1 Peter 4:12–19
Temptation	Luke 4:1–13; 1 Corinthians 10:13
Thought Life	Colossians 3:1–11
Tongue	James 3:1–12
Trials	Psalm 40; James 1:12–18
Worldliness	James 4:1–6
Worry	Matthew 6:25–34; Philippians 4:6–7; 1 Peter 5:6–7

spirit" (Hebrews 4:12), it does not need to be at the front of our conscious minds in order to do its work. Scripture—particularly when we are exposed to it for prolonged periods, such as meditation—penetrates to a deeper level and works there.

Many years ago, an elderly man complained to his pastor, who had urged upon him a program of Scripture memory. "I don't think it's working. It doesn't matter how much I review. It's like pouring water into a sieve. I just don't keep any of it."

His pastor was equal to the moment: "Yes, but at least you have a clean sieve."

Remember that the meditation process is interaction with God using the Word as the medium. We read, we reflect, we respond. That process itself is what matters. Being able to repeat Scripture verbatim does not *necessarily* produce anything worthwhile. The Bible must become a medium of interaction with God, a springboard to knowing Him better. Otherwise, not much happens.

Bill Gates, president of Microsoft Corporation, is one of the world's richest men. When Bill was eleven, his pastor, Dale Turner, challenged the congregation to memorize the Sermon on the Mount. Dale promised that any who could repeat it exactly would be treated to dinner at a plush Seattle restaurant. Gates proceeded to memorize the entire sermon during a two-and-a-half-hour drive with his parents. After reciting the lengthy passage to Pastor Turner, Gates said, "I can do anything I put my mind to."

Yet when asked a few years ago if he believed in God, Gates told a reporter, "Oh, I guess, agnostic, atheist, I must be one of those." He later said, "Well, it might sound better to call me a Protestant who hasn't gone to church in a while."[3]

There is nothing magical about memorizing Scripture. Unless it is a means to a godly end, memorizing can be just another opportunity to display our pride; like Bill Gates, our memorizing a Bible passage won't necessarily lead us closer to God. For the person who genuinely wants to know God better, however, Scripture memory is priceless, because it allows the relational process to go on "day and night" (Psalm 1:2; Joshua 1:8).

Regularly hiding the Word in one's heart will keep you from sin. Seminary president and veteran pastor Charles Swindoll once explained its power to protect:

> I was in Canada. . . . I had been away from home eight days, and there were two more to go—a weekend. I was lonely and having a pity-party for myself at supper—alone. I bought a newspaper, thumbed through the sports section, and found nothing but hockey—the favorite of Canadians, but not mine. I heaved a sigh and walked toward the elevator. En route, I heard a couple of young women talking and laughing as they used the hotel phone in the lobby.
>
> I smiled as I passed by and a few steps later punched the "up" elevator button. I got on. So did the two ladies. I punched "6." They didn't reach for the row of buttons, so I asked, "What floor?" One looked at me rather sensually and said, "How about six? Do you have any plans?"
>
> We were all alone on an elevator. In Canada . . . These women were available, and I was lonely . . .
>
> Do you know what immediately flashed into my mind? My wife and four children? No, not at first. My position and reputation? No, not then. The possibility of being seen or set up? No.
>
> God gave me a visual instant replay of Galatians 6:7, "Do not be deceived. God is not mocked; for whatever a man sows, this he will also reap."
>
> And Ephesians 6:11, "Put on the full armor of God, that you may be able to stand firm against the schemes of the devil. . . ."
>
> During that elevator lift, the memorized Word flew to my rescue. Right on time.
>
> As I looked back at the two, I replied, "I've got a full evening planned already; I'm really not interested." They looked at me like I was Mork from Ork as I stepped off the elevator (and they stayed on!) . . . Yes, the memorized Word works.[4]

SOME DECISIONS ABOUT MEMORIZING

Once you decide to memorize Scripture as part of your meditation, certain decisions must be made. The first decision is what verse(s) to memorize.

What to Memorize

In many ways, choosing what to memorize is a simple and

"no-lose" decision. There is nothing wrong, however, with being systematic about it. The simplest approach is to memorize some or all of a passage you are meditating on. If you are working your way through a book, select a verse or two from each week's segment of the book under study.

Another sound method is to meditate and memorize based on a current spiritual challenge. Having trouble with your tongue? Begin in James 3. Discouraged? Start with Psalm 27.

A listing of problem-oriented passages is included in the "Meditation Close-up" earlier in this chapter if you want to proceed this way. You can find others in a topical Bible. Don't try to memorize an entire section all at once. Proceed at a comfortable pace.

Another avenue of memory work is to memorize based on maximizing the variety of your personal study. Spend time in narrative material (Genesis, Mark, Acts) one month; in the Epistles (letters by the apostles, from Romans through Jude) a second month; and in Old Testament poetry the next. Just because the books of the Bible appear in a certain order is no reason to memorize them that way.

Still another approach is to memorize in connection with ministry. Are you teaching a Sunday school class in Mark? Your class will be the better for it if you memorize from and meditate on this week's lesson.

There are some intrinsic dangers to this approach, of course. It is possible to fall into the trap of merely seeing the Bible as the solution to other people's spiritual needs if your sole concern is ministry. If you want to memorize in connection with ministry, apply it to yourself first. Share with those you serve the overflow of your own heart, and God's purposes will be fulfilled. Also, be sure not to limit your study of Scripture to the lessons you are preparing—at least for very long.

How Much to Memorize

Second, decide how much you want to memorize. Most people can memorize effectively and easily enough in chunks of one to four verses per week. The key words in that sentence are *most people.* If it takes you two weeks to do one verse, so be it. At the end of the year you will have memorized twenty-six verses. At the end of five years, your inner being will have been exposed to 130. If you meditate faithfully on those verses, the spiritual changes will be noticeable to you and those around you.

When to Memorize

Third, decide when to memorize. Most Christians have more time for memory work than they think. Thanks to some of our modern customs (such as driving, riding the bus or commuter train, and standing in line), we can redeem the time (see Ephesians 5:15–16) in a comparatively painless fashion. Keeping a three-by-five-inch card with you inscribed with this week's memory verse(s) will enable you to hide God's Word in your heart and get going in the meditation process. My wife, Cheryl, often tapes her 3x5 memory cards at strategic places around the house so that they will be there to remind her to spend a few minutes memorizing and meditating.

If you have a long commute each day, that's a natural time to make some spiritual hay; an audio recording of your verses works as well as cards (see next section). If you take walks for exercise, take a tape and your Walkman with you and memorize along the way. Do your walking on a treadmill? Put a 3x5 card in front of you and accomplish two tasks at once. There are lots of opportunities available; if you really want to memorize, you can.

Everybody has to fight the time battle. If you carefully analyze the flow of your week, however, you will find that somewhere in that 168-hour span quite a few minutes are just waiting for you. You won't find a better way to use them.

How to Memorize

Methods of memorizing abound. The options below may be combined for maximum effectiveness.

Repeated reading. Some people find that simply repeating the reading of the text they are meditating on is all they need to gain working control of it. Doing it this way usually works better when the text is read aloud.

Listening. One painless way of memorizing is to read the text onto a cassette tape and replay it in your car on the way to work. Read a verse onto the tape, then allow a gap of time long enough to repeat the verse. Do it again fifteen or twenty times (you'll be learning the passage as you do this). Put the tape into your cassette player and you are ready to do some serious memory work. You will also find that traffic jams become far less burdensome.

You can buy commercially produced tapes of professional speakers reciting the Old Testament or New Testament, but these recordings are more valuable for extensive exposure than they are for meditation. For your memory work, concentrate on bite-size portions.

Writing. An often overlooked means of memorizing is writing out the text, a practice that was a moral obligation for the kings of Israel. As Moses was preparing Israel to transit the Jordan and fight for the land, he explained that it was just a matter of time before the people asked for a king. What should the new leader do to prepare himself for his weighty responsibilities?

> He shall write for himself a copy of this law in a book, from the one before the priests, the Levites. And it shall be with him, and he shall read it all the days of his life, that he may learn to fear the Lord his God and be careful to observe all the words of this law and these statutes, that his heart may not be lifted above his brethren, that he may not turn aside from the commandment to the right hand or to the left, and that he may prolong his days in his kingdom, he and his children in the midst of Israel. (Deuteronomy 17:18–20)

Writing out the text forces us to slow down and deal with it a word at a time. It frequently is the most effective step in memorizing, and one I have found to be particularly helpful.

Review. Keep a few index cards handy with your current memory verse and any others you want to review. When standing in line, pull out the cards and review them. Better still, hand the cards to a friend and have him check your retention. You may even get another person involved in the process!

When we become serious about memorizing Scripture—and have a plan to do it—we will get to know the author of the Word of

God better. And knowing God is a major goal of true meditation.

MEDITATIONS IN HIS WORD

Realize

Read Psalm 90.

Who wrote this psalm? Do you see any significance in that in the light of its content?

Retain

Memorize Psalm 90:12.

Reflect

1. In what sense is God the "dwelling place" of believers? Does this statement lend credence to the eastern concept that humans are "one with the Godhead"?

2. Moses lived through the death of an entire generation of Israelites. About one and a quarter million people perished in the wilderness over the span of forty years. How did that experience qualify him to write the words of this psalm?

3. Does verse 14 address the recurring issue of man's dissatisfaction with life? What truly satisfies the human heart?

Respond

1. Have you been seeking satisfaction of your longings in ways that are not suitable for a Christian?

2. In what ways will you begin to redeem your time on the basis of this passage?

Friends often say, "I have so much to do, so many people to see, I cannot find time for Scripture study." Perhaps there are not many who have more to do than I. For more than half a century I have never known one day when I had not more business than I could get through. For 4 years I have had annually about 30,000 letters, and most of these have passed through my own hands.

Then, as pastor of a church with 1,200 believers, great has been my care. Besides, I have had charge of five immense orphanages; also, at my publishing depot, the printing and circulating of millions of tracts, books and Bibles; but I have always made it a rule never to begin work until I have had a good season with God and His Word.

—George Mueller

CHAPTER 8

Reflecting on God's Truth

For years George Goble, a computer specialist in the engineering department at Purdue University in West Lafayette, Indiana, and his fellow engineers have held regular barbecues at a local park. They meet to enjoy good food in relaxing surroundings. They are, however, engineers; and one summer day their inquisitive minds began to speculate, as they waited for their charcoal to be ready for cooking, if they could speed up that process.

Goble later told a reporter what happened: "We started by blowing the charcoal with a hair dryer. . . . Then we figured out that it would light faster if we used a vacuum cleaner." Being engineers, the men forgot about cooking the hamburgers and focused on seeing how fast they could ignite the charcoal. They began using a vacuum cleaner; then they graduated to a propane torch, followed by an acetylene torch. Next came compressed pure oxygen. Now the charcoal was lighting very quickly, as one might expect, since fire comes about from oxygen being mixed with some reducing agent, such as wood or charcoal. Columnist Dave Barry, who recounted the story, noted what happened next:

By this point, Goble was getting pretty good times. But in the world of competitive charcoal-lighting, "pretty good" does not cut the mustard.

Thus, Goble hit upon the idea of using—get ready—liquid oxygen. This is the form of oxygen used in rocket engines; it's 295 degrees below zero and 600 times as dense as regular oxygen. In terms of releasing energy, pouring liquid oxygen on charcoal is the equivalent of throwing a live squirrel into a room containing 50 million Labrador retrievers. . . .

What follows is the most impressive charcoal-lighting I have ever seen [the event is shown on Goble's own computer web site], featuring a large fireball that, according to Goble, reached 10,000 degrees Fahrenheit. The charcoal was ready for cooking in—this has to be a world record—3 seconds. [1]

Our modern concern for haste does produce its casualties, far worse than losing the simple pleasures of waiting for the charcoal to turn white. Common among the losses is time for quiet reflection. Meditation produces few mushroom clouds, but it works in the unseen realms where nuclear devices are pitifully weak.

Modern culture's preference for the harried moment will not benefit you in the quest for meditation. Reflection can't be hurried. You will have to make it happen by taking a few critical steps: set a time, get a place, use your imagination and your memory, and give God's truth due consideration.

SETTING A TIME

Though meditation, including reflection, can be done any time, having a regular time (and place) works best for most people. The old hymn "Take Time to Be Holy" may occasionally be sung in our churches, but it is commonly ignored in our schedules. Meditation requires taking time to be with God.

Mornings worked best for King David. He wrote, "Early will I seek You" (Psalm 63:1). In Psalm 5:2–3, he urged God to hear his morning cries: "Give heed to the voice of my cry, my King and my God, for to You I will pray. My voice You shall hear in the morning, O Lord; In the morning I will direct it to You, and I will look up."

Daniel met with God frequently. "Daniel . . . knelt down on his knees three times that day, and prayed and gave thanks before his God, as was his custom since early days" (Daniel 6:10). The last phrase is instructive. Daniel met with God three times daily not because Scripture required it, but because it was a well-established personal practice.

The best time for you may be different. The end of the day works better for some believers. For young mothers, those rare quiet moments when Junior goes down for his afternoon nap will probably be the best (and possibly the only) time they can meet with God.

A particular time is almost always a necessity. However, the godly person's "delight is in the law of the Lord, and in His law he meditates day and night" (Psalm 1:2). Intermittent meditation comes from delighting in the Word. The one who finds joy in God's Word will find a way. This may require creativity. One Bible teacher I know worked his way through seminary by operating a stamp press, a machine that required little concentration. To make the most of his time, he rose early enough each day to memorize one verse of Scripture to take to work with him. During the day, while performing his work responsibilities, he meditated on that one verse. At the end of the day, he would return home and write down his insights in a small journal, building not only his life but a foundation for future ministry as well.

So what is the "right" way? There isn't one right time; however, remember that in the Scriptures, those who met regularly with God were dedicating a strategic portion of their day to God. God instructed Israel to offer Him the firstfruits of each crop as a symbol of their thanksgiving. It seems logical that He likewise deserves the best part of our day, whenever it may be.

GETTING A PLACE

Reflection is easier if you have a special place set aside in which to do it. Showing up at the office a few minutes early and closing the door may be all you need. (The early travel time may help you miss the traffic too). Or, your living room couch may work better. Significantly, the place you choose should be private.

Reading and studying the text should not occupy the whole

time you have to meet with God. Remember that you will also want to respond to what you are learning by entering into worship, thanksgiving, and intercession. It is thinking about what you read and study, however, that will bring you to the point of responding. Howard Hendricks insists, "You're reading too much if you reflect on it too little."[2] (I will have more to say about responding to God on the basis of your reflection in chapter 9.) With that in mind, find a quiet place, away from visual or audio distractions. God and His Word deserve your full, focused attention.

USING YOUR IMAGINATION

Some people claim—amazingly, in my judgment—that the Bible bores them. Yet the Scriptures resound with the clash of armies as nations and empires rise and fall. It is filled with conspiracy, intrigue, mystery, and godly passion. As you reflect on God's truth, you can participate in these exciting scenes. Your imagination can become a means of appreciating the importance of the issues at stake. Using the imagination helps clarify the commonality of experience between biblical people and yourself.

The great Victorian preacher, Alexander Whyte, saw its value: "Do not be afraid at the word 'imagination,' my brethren. It has been sadly ill-used, both name and thing. But it is a noble name and a noble thing. There is nothing so noble in all that is within us."[3] Using the imagination can follow several paths.

Put Yourself into the Role of the Human Authors

Paul must have felt terribly grieved when he was compelled to write the troublesome believers in Corinth in an effort to defend his own apostleship. He had led them to Christ, taught them, prayed for them, and nurtured them through one crisis after another. In return, they questioned his credentials and refused to support him financially. If you are reading 2 Corinthians 10:1–18, imagine Paul's feelings. Do you ever feel unappreciated? If you have, you will identify with Paul's defense of himself in Second Corinthians. Perhaps you have a friend who has done much at work yet receives little respect. Imagine him as Paul, and the passage comes alive.

Do you know what it feels like to fail morally in the public eye? I hope not. The best way to know the sorrow and humiliation of that situation, however, is to read David's account of his experience. Psalms 32 and 51 reveal the horror of sin in its personal effects and its bearing on one's relationship to God.

Put Yourself into the Role of the Divine Author

Imagining ourselves in Jesus' sandals may seem impossible. Indeed, there are limits to what we fallen humans can do in this respect, but as we read the gospel accounts we can enter into at least some of Jesus' pain in Gethsemane. We may also understand some of God's pain when His own dear Son later was abused and killed. By reflecting on how we would feel were we in Jesus' position, we can appreciate the disappointment we have caused Him as well. After all, He suffered for us.

We read in Matthew how Peter asked Jesus to let him join the Master as he walked on the Sea of Galilee: "'Lord, if it is You, command me to come to You on the water.' So He said, 'Come.'" (Matthew 14:28–29). Imagine the scene. For months you have been encouraging your small band of disciples to learn to trust God and take Him at His Word. Now one of them is asking for an opportunity to do just that. Would you be cautious or enthusiastic in your response to this small step on Peter's part? "Come!" is a cry of joy, we may be sure; it certainly encourages those of us who are reluctant to trust Him for anything out of the ordinary.

Our imagination might picture a weary smile on the face of our Lord as He explains to the disciples, "I must journey today, tomorrow, and the day following; for it cannot be that a prophet should perish outside of Jerusalem" (Luke 13:33). Since the Bible has no laugh track, its humor can be easily missed, and to our detriment. As we place ourselves into the text by using our imaginations, we will be more able to notice the flavor of the biblical account as well as its vocabulary.

Put Yourself into the Crowd

Crowds usually don't come off well in the pages of Scripture. By using our imaginations to place ourselves in the crowds of Scripture, we can accomplish two worthwhile objectives. First, we can appreciate the force of those temptations that lead believers to conform rather than stand firm; second, we can begin to think through our own responses to the daily pressures we face.

For example, you can develop more spiritual independence by imagining the scene before Pilate's tribunal, as the multitude was bought off by the religious leaders. How would you have responded if you had been approached by a priestly dignitary and urged to call for Jesus' blood? Would you have quietly acquiesced or openly resisted?

Imagination helps us feel the carnal pull in David's heart as his advisors whispered that he should kill Saul when the latter was within his grasp. If you had been part of his entourage, how would you have advised him?

While reading in the book of Numbers, our reflecting can lead us to feel and abhor the mindlessness of the people as Israel rebelled against Moses. If you had been eating manna for months—boiled, fried, fricasseed, poached, or baked—would you have resisted the pressure to call for something else to eat? Could you have opposed the crowd's strange twisting of history (Numbers 11:5–6) to justify their cravings?

A holy imagination helps us to recognize and anticipate some of the common dangers of going along with the crowd.

Put Yourself into the Role of the Protagonist

It may be hard to relate to the apostle Paul's travails of soul, but many a person can picture himself as a Gideon. The unassuming attitude of this individual ("Who? Me? Deliver Israel?") can capture our minds and lifts before us the possibility that God can use us too.

Your imagination can bring you into the pain of Aaron, who was forbidden to mourn for his sons by the Lord, since they had profaned the tabernacle. After Nadab and Abihu were violently destroyed by God, Moses told Aaron and the remaining sons, "Do not uncover your heads nor tear your clothes, lest you die, and wrath come upon all the people. But let your brethren, the whole house of Israel, bewail the burning which the Lord has kindled" (Leviticus 10:6). Think of the possible loss of your own child (or, if childless, of a friend's child). Such a ban against mourning this personal loss would leave you with deep pain, perhaps frustration. Aaron discovered that there were aspects to priestly ministry which he had not anticipated. So will we.

USING YOUR MEMORY

Memory is one of God's most important tools in our lives. Lots of celebrations in Scripture were built around remembering: the Passover celebration, the Feast of Tabernacles, the Day of Atonement, and of course, supremely, the Lord's Table, that variation on the Passover that centers on the words, "Do this in remembrance of Me." Israel's calendar was so full of festivals that they could never go for more than a few months without having some reason to slow down and remember what God had done for them.

In Deuteronomy 6:10–11, Moses promised Israel that when they conquered the land, God would give them "large and beautiful cities which you did not build, houses full of all good things, which you did not fill, hewn-out wells which you did not dig, vineyards and olive trees which you did not plant." Then comes the punch line: "When you have eaten and are full—then beware, lest you forget the Lord" (Deuteronomy 6:12).

When does the danger come? "When you have eaten and are full."

Mark it well: the greatest dangers to your spiritual life occur not in the midst of the battle, but after the conflict is over and you begin to enjoy the fruits of victory. Those dangers are not external, but internal: "Beware, lest you forget the Lord." Meditating regularly upon the truths of Scripture and upon His grace in your own life will minimize the likelihood of forgetting Him.

Of course, people do not forget the Lord in the absolute sense. If you had approached an Israelite after the people conquered the land and said, "Tell me, who is your God?" he would have had no trouble remembering God's name. It is not absence from one's knowledge that is the problem. It is absence from one's preoccupation. God doesn't vanish from our memories; He disappears from our conscious thought moment by moment. Meditation helps us keep reminding ourselves that all that we are and have are due to His grace and kindness. Fail to do so and we begin to drift away, a little at a time. Reflection ought to include the process of remembering intentionally, with the Scriptures serving to spur us in the proper direction.

God anticipated Israel's forgetfulness in spiritual matters. In Numbers 15:38–39, He said, "Speak to the children of Israel: Tell them to make tassels on the corners of their garments throughout their generations, and to put a blue thread in the tassels of the corners . . . that you may look upon it and remember all the commandments of the Lord and do them." Here was a tangible way to keep the Lord in their memories: The tassels would remind them to consider the truth as contained in His commandments. How often were they reminded? As often as they wore clothes. The memory in the believer ought always to serve as a deterrent to spiritual drift.

Unfortunately, Israel subsequently ignored God's wise counsel. The people forgot about God. Consider Judges, the most unusual book in the Old Testament. Israel gets into more trouble spiritually and does more insane things in Judges than in any book of Scripture. Why did it happen? Judges 8:34 explains, "The children of Israel did not remember the Lord their God, who had delivered them from the hands of all their enemies on every side." They went about their business without giving Him a thought. By contrast, the psalmist says of his own meditation, "I remember Your name in the night, O Lord, and I keep Your law" (Psalm 119:55). The first (remembering) makes the second (keeping) possible.

CONSIDERING GOD'S TRUTH

The psalmist says, "The wicked wait for me to destroy me, but I will consider your testimonies" (Psalm 119:95). Here's a question worth some thought: If you knew that a group of people were out either to discredit or to kill you, and you had a limited amount of time to prepare for the event, what would you do? We see from this verse a godly person's priorities. Considering God's truth is a way to use limited time for maximum profit.

A Definition of Considering

The word that is translated *consider* in Psalm 119:95 is the Hebrew verb *bin* (pronounced *bean*). The term appears 170 times in the

Old Testament and is usually translated "be prudent" or "discern." The root idea beneath it is differentiation or separation. The "considering" person thinks things through and is able to distinguish between important factors and secondary ones.

David possessed the quality in great abundance. One of the first descriptions of him in the Bible comes from the mouth of one of Saul's royal counselors: "I have seen a son of Jesse the Bethlehemite, who is skillful in playing, a mighty man of valor, a man of war, prudent in speech, and a handsome person; and the Lord is with him" (1 Samuel 16:18). The relevant word is *prudent*. David's thinking was always in gear before his mouth opened; he *considered* before he spoke.

These verses and passages like them give us a basis for a definition of "considering." To consider is *to think through the implications of God's truth, and then make the choices those implications dictate*. As such, it forms an important part of meditation.

What We Consider: God's Truth

Notice that it is God's truth that is the object of consideration, not simply Scripture, although that is the heart of God's truth. The person who considers has his eyes open toward all the realities that God has either established or permitted. Reflection is a time not only to imagine things as they were, but to consider things as they are—and ought to be.

One implication of this definition is that "considering" is not simply a mental phenomenon; it is moral as well. The reason for this is that in almost every important decision you will ever make you will be able to find reasons against making the right decision. It will not only take insight, it will take courage to make the best choice.

Considering God's truth is best done in a contemplative environment. Solitude is a help. Perhaps the lack of these conditions explains why our generation often makes unwise choices. We don't push aside some of the things we want to do—or worse, think we are entitled to do—in order to have a quiet environment to consider our lives in the light of God's Word.

Some Examples of "Considering"

Certain themes are commended to us in the Bible as worthy of extended consideration. These timeless matters apply to believers across the board.

Considering what is important (Psalm 8:3–4). David provides a wonderful example of the process of considering God's truth because he possessed all the time constraints that you and I do and then some. In his youth, he was on the run from Saul for years. When he came to maturity, he faced the demands of trying to unite an unruly collection of tribes. In spite of these challenges, he made room in his schedule for quiet contemplation.

During his kingship, he wrote the lovely words, "When I consider Your heavens, the work of Your fingers, the moon and the stars, which You have ordained, what is man that You are mindful of him, and the son of man that You visit him?" (Psalm 8:3–4). As he sat looking at the skies at night, certain truths occurred to him. God's creative power and energy are vast, much more than he could comprehend. Man seemed a small part of it all, yet he clearly is the focus of God's concern.

From these basic facts David considered an implication: If God possesses such power and creativity, why would He spend time thinking about the one portion of His creation which opposes Him? Why would He expend effort involving himself in human affairs? He didn't say so, but the alternative was on the tip of David's tongue: Why not just destroy mankind and be done with it? God involves Himself with man because He has chosen to love what He has made and to save at least some of us from oblivion.

From looking at the night sky and giving it extended thought, David had arrived at certain conclusions about God's dealings with man: His actions are all born of His grace and His love.

Now you may say, "That's a lot to draw out of a quiet night just looking up at the sky." I don't think so. These are the only conclusions that may be reached; but a lot of people never reach them; they have more pressing things to consider.

I have discovered through frustrating experience that it is incredibly difficult to convince people that God loves them. There are many reasons for that, not the least of which is that Satan, the enemy of souls, will do everything in his power to confuse them about the issue. He knows that once you convince a person that God loves him, he is very close to the kingdom of God. The gospel makes sense then. The Cross seems both logical and necessary.

The Bible itself makes a great deal of this. When you read Psalm 8, you are only a short conceptual distance from Romans 5:8: "God demonstrates His own love toward us, in that while we were still sinners, Christ died for us." If there are evidences of God's love and grace even in the skies, then it stands to reason that He might do something remarkable, like become a man and die for our sins. It is worth thinking about.

Considering what is rational (Isaiah 1:3). Another topic worth considering is thoughts about God. When we consider how much we depend upon God for our very breath, we see the irrationality of living without giving Him a thought. At the very outset of his *magnum opus,* Isaiah conveys God's mournful words about His people in Judah and Jerusalem: "The ox knows its owner and the donkey its master's crib; but Israel does not know, My people do not *consider"* (Isaiah 1:3). There's that word again, this time in a negative context. Judah refused to allow God's truth to guide their decisions.

Even dumb animals value those who provide their food. Judah drew its every breath from God's grace; in return, they bowed down to idols. They did not take time to think through the implications of God's ownership. Have you considered who owns you? Does that consideration enter into the crucial decisions you make?

Recognizing God's ownership is only part of thinking about a rational response to God. Paul said that offering our bodies to God for His service is a logical and rational response to His mercies (Romans 12:1). He also insisted that the death of Christ leads to the rational decision to live not for ourselves, but for Him who died for us (2 Corinthians 5:14–15). Spiritual living is rational living.

Considering relative values (Romans 8:18). Our troubles seem weighty now, but how trivial they are when we consider what is stored up for us for the future! We spend an enormous amount of time coping with our pains. Lots of energy goes into helping us adjust to our limitations. You and I both know people who are consumed with their sufferings, who never allow the opportunity to pass without telling us how terrible are the agonies they endure.

The insightful person, the person who considers, will have none of that. He is conscious of his pains, but they don't occupy much of his mind. Paul is a classic case in point: He said, "I consider that the sufferings of this present time are not worthy to be compared with the glory which shall be revealed in us" (Romans 8:18).

That's a healthy way to think about hardships. No words of denial for Paul. We are not to try to push our difficulties into some corner of our minds where they won't bother us. What we are supposed to do is to think the whole business through. Our sufferings are real, but they're trivial in comparison with what God has planned for us. But the full extent of what He has planned is conditional, as Paul says earlier in the context, upon *obedient* suffering. Our difficulties, if we respond to them properly, have the present benefit of producing beauty in us; but compared to the glories of the age to come they are nothing.

Considering your personal difficulties (Hebrews 12:3). One of the greatest exercises available to the believer is considering the life of the Lord Jesus Himself. That is what the writer of the letter to the Hebrews had in mind when he wrote, "Consider Him who endured such hostility from sinners against Himself, lest you become weary and discouraged in your souls" (Hebrews 12:3). Remembering the awful hostility that the Lord Jesus endured for me helps to place in perspective the momentary bumps of my life now. Considering Him helps us realize the truth of what Warren Wiersbe is fond of saying: "The bumps are what you climb on."

The Lord Jesus knew what hostility was, yet He pressed ahead with the work He had to do. Never has anyone had so many reasons to be discouraged and throw in the towel. But He didn't. He took all the world had to offer Him and kept moving toward His objectives.

Someone asked then President Dwight Eisenhower who was the greatest among all the great men he knew. He answered, "The greatest person I have ever known wasn't a man. It was a woman, my mother." He described her as both a smart and saintly lady. "Often in this job I have wished I could consult her about questions, particularly about people. But she is in heaven. However, I knew her mind so well that many times I have felt I knew what she would say."

One night in their farm home, Mrs. Eisenhower was playing a card game with her boys. "Now, don't get me wrong," said the former president, "it was not with those cards that have kings, queens, jacks, and spades on them. Mother was too straitlaced for that." President Eisenhower said the game they were playing was called Flinch.

"Anyway, Mother was the dealer, and she dealt me a very bad hand. I began to complain. Mother said, 'Boys, put down your cards. I want to say something, particularly to Dwight. You are in a game in your home with your mother and brothers who love you. But out in the world you will be dealt bad hands without love. Here is some advice for you boys. Take those bad hands without complaining and play them out. Ask God to help you, and you will win the important game called life.'" The president added, "I've tried to follow that wise advice always."[4]

How do we respond to difficulties properly? Not by complaining, that's for sure. I have probably spent more time in my personal Bible study in the Gospels than in any other section. As I read those amazing documents telling the story of the earthly life of Christ, I am struck by the Savior's total lack of grumbling. The closest thing I have ever found to a complaint occurred on the night of His arrest. Then He said, "My soul is exceedingly sorrowful, even to death." The only other example was what He said a short time later as He prayed alone in Gethsemane. Suffering by Himself, He rebuked his three sleeping friends, saying, "Could you not watch with Me one hour?"

They should have been awake to do some reflecting—being alert to consider the implications of what was about to happen and to support their Master in prayer. Instead, they were causing the Lord Jesus grief, because they failed to suffer with Him.

The long and the short of it: We need to consider God's truth. We need to do so in an unhurried fashion, to be awake with Him for one hour and think about the price He paid to redeem us. We need to think through the implications of that and make our life's decisions accordingly.

BE PATIENT

Remember as you become involved in the process that meditation isn't supposed to yield remarkable insights and dramatic changes every day. In many respects, its most important consequences happen so slowly that we don't see them at all for a while. You do the reflecting, and let God's Spirit do the inner reworking in your heart. That is His specialty.

Take time to be holy.

MEDITATIONS IN HIS WORD

Realize

Read Revelation 2:1–7.

Retain

Memorize Revelation 2:5.

Reflect

1. The Lord Jesus finds the loss of the Ephesian believers' first love disturbing. Do you think He refers to their love for Him or their love for others? Is it necessary to choose between these?

2. The church at Ephesus is commended here for their concern for truth, yet rebuked for diminished love. In your experience, is this a common combination? Why do you think the two so often are seen alongside each other?

3. Using the content of the letter, make a brief list (in your own words) of ways to recognize a condition of diminished love in your own life, or in the life of anyone.

4. The three commands of verse 5 give a three-step process for recovering from a loss of first love. The third of these ("do the first works") helps to define the role of godly actions in reviving love for Christ and for others. Do actions produce love, or does love produce action— or are both ideas true?

Respond

1. How would you assess the state of your love toward Christ? Toward people? Is it as great as it was when you first became a believer in the Lord Jesus?

2. What are some specific steps you will take today to energize your love for Christ and others?

Mind is the highest thing, and meditation is the highest use of mind; it is the true root, and sap, and fatness of all faith and prayer and spiritual obedience. Why are our minds so blighted and so barren in the things of God? Why have we so little faith? Why have we so little hold of the reality and nobility of Divine things? The reason is plain—we seldom or never meditate. We read our New Testament, on occasion, and we hear it read, but we do not take time to meditate. We pray sometimes, or we pretend to pray; but do we ever set ourselves to prepare our hearts for the mercy-seat by strenuous meditation on who and what we are; on who and what He is to whom we pretend to pray; and on what it is we are to say, and do, and ask, and receive?

—Alexander Whyte

CHAPTER 9

Responding to God's Truth

Don't become unduly focused on the mechanics of meditation. Such advice may sound strange, given the subject of the book, but the warning is essential. Meditation is not an end in itself; it's a means of carrying on a personal relationship. And relationships function best when the people involved concentrate on each other rather than on the methods and rules by which they relate.

Relating to God has much in common with relating to people, but it differs in critical ways too—the most obvious one being that God is physically absent, though personally present. That's a major reason we have many word pictures in Scripture describing how God and man can relate. Probably the most common is that of a Father and His children. Others include a Teacher and His disciples, a Shepherd and His sheep, a King and His subjects (and for those who prove faithful, His friends), a Head and its body. No one model suffices to encompass our relationship to Him, since God's personality is so multifaceted. These word pictures suggest God's glory and awesome nature. (They also form excellent subjects for meditation, by the way.)

After thinking deeply on the Lord and His Word, however, you will want to respond to Him in a manner that is in keeping with who He is and what He has been teaching you in the Word. The apostle Paul, after reflecting on God's mercies in an extended way (for eleven chapters, in fact), urged Roman believers: "I beseech you therefore, brethren, by the mercies of God, that you present your bodies a living sacrifice, holy, acceptable to God, which is your reasonable service" (Romans 12:1). As someone has observed, the trouble with a living sacrifice is that it keeps crawling off the altar. Responding properly to God as you meditate will help weave the ropes that will minimize this problem.

THE RESPONSE OF THE SINNING BELIEVER

In our meditations, the first response, logically speaking, is confession. The apostle John, intimate friend of Jesus Christ, included himself when he wrote, "If we confess our sins, He is faithful and just to forgive us our sins and to cleanse us from all unrighteousness" (1 John 1:9). The forgiveness in question has nothing to do with qualifying us for eternal life. John assumed the eternal life of his readers throughout his letter (1 John 2:7, 12–14; 5:13). Confessing our sins is a purely relational act; it affects the present relationship. You cannot sin as His child and then proceed with the relationship as though nothing had happened. That would be a denial of reality.

Confession is my acknowledgment to God that I have sinned. It is often accompanied by remorse, although the two are not identical. Remorse is the emotional regret that naturally accompanies injuring someone you love. Confession is the step that reopens communication with the injured party.

The importance of confession is seen in an episode from the days of the Israelite conquest. After Israel's defeat at Ai, Joshua was lying prone in earnest prayer before God, pouring out his heart. Israel had just lost a battle. *What was happening?* Joshua wondered.

Yet in the midst of his prayer for his people, this godly man was rebuked. God declared: "Get up! Why do you lie thus on your face? Israel has sinned" (Joshua 7:10–11). When there is unconfessed sin in the camp, it is not time to offer supplications. Thanksgiving will have to wait; offerings can be made later. Confession has the priority. Once the decks are clear of wreckage, the ship can proceed.

Within the familiar words of 1 John 1:9 lies a truth worthy of special note. As the Holy Spirit brings our sins to our conscious minds, it is our responsibility to acknowledge them. When we do so, God forgives not only those sins we confess, but *all* unrighteousness. Absolutely nothing then stands in the way of our communication.

The uncomfortable truth is that none of us is fully aware of all the things we do that grieve the Lord. In His grace, God breaks it to us gently and gradually that we still have a lot of growing to do. In *Mere Christianity*, C. S. Lewis describes how growth and awareness of our frailty accompany each other:

> When a man is getting better, he understands more and more clearly the evil that still is left in him. When a man is getting worse, he understands his own badness less and less. A moderately bad man knows he is not very good; a thoroughly bad man thinks he is all right. This is common sense, really. You understand sleep when you are awake, not while you are sleeping.... You can understand the nature of drunkenness when you are sober, not when you are drunk. Good people know about both good and evil: bad people do not know about either.[1]

It is when sins are confessed and openness is restored that other responses come into play.

THE RESPONSE OF THE HAPPY BELIEVER

The more we meditate on God's Word, the more we discover how much we are blessed (happy). In fact, it is our duty to be happy people and to return worship and thanksgiving to God from that happiness. Almost every exhortation in Scripture to worship God is attached to words which promote exuberance. Consider Psalm 95:1–2: "Oh come, let us sing to the Lord! Let us shout joyfully to the Rock of our salvation. Let us come before His presence with thanksgiving; let us shout joyfully to Him with psalms."

You cannot properly render worship to God without your affections and your emotions being involved—and that raises an interesting and useful paradox. On the one hand, God wants us to be joyful in worship. On the other hand, we cannot coerce our emotions into doing our bidding.

Not that people haven't tried. The results, however, inevitably prove unconvincing. Church leaders sometimes attempt to engineer public worship in such a way that they force others into being joyful. That doesn't usually work, either. God knows whether joy is really present (whether in a heart or in a worship service), and it does make a difference to Him.

To understand why, you only have to remember that in any love relationship, *rejoicing in the beloved is the basis of honor.* When a wife receives an anniversary present from her husband, she may ask, "Why did you do this?"

As every husband knows, that's an important question.

If her mate replies, "I was obliged to do so by custom—it's our anniversary," it is an insult to her (and it could result in injury to him). On the other hand, if he says, "You are the joy of my life; I just had to honor you with something nice," her response will be quite different. Delighting in the relationship is the basis of a good marriage; it's also the basis of all genuine worship of God.

Remember the paradox: God wants us to be joyful, yet we cannot force our emotions to be exuberant—and if we could, it would mean little. So what is the solution to this dilemma? The answer is very simple: You must bring an *existing joy* to worship with you. You cannot wait to suddenly be joyous when you approach God in public worship. You cannot turn on joyful worship when Sunday morning comes if you have ignored God all week.

"Rejoice always" (Philippians 4:4) is the motto written on the banner of Christian living. Getting in touch with God *every day* in meditation will help keep you conscious of the many reasons to be glad in Him.

Another way of expressing joy is found in the psalmist's invitation: "Delight yourself also in the Lord, and He shall give you the desires of your heart" (Psalm 37:4). You find the expression "delighting in the Lord," popping up periodically in Scripture. It summarizes the logical end of meditation. Notice that it has a promise attached: "He shall give you the desires of your heart."

What an incredible and gracious incentive! *The desires of your heart.* Another way of saying this is: "all that you could ever want."

Meditation
Close-up
Responding to God

Meditation ought not to be self-absorbed. It is, after all, a means of relating to a Person, and relationships function best when people are more concerned about each other than about the rules that govern their relationship. The meditating believer will generally respond to God in ways that reflect his awareness and appreciation of God's unique Person.

- When we discover that we have disobeyed, we will confess our sins.

- As our awareness of our blessed condition increases, we will become increasingly joyful people.

- An increasing Christlikeness will cause us to be intercessors for others.

- Meditation will make us obedient, or disobedience will ruin our meditation.

What is the means of gaining this remarkable set of blessings? Delighting in the Lord. The word *delight* used in Psalm 37:4 occurs only ten times in the Hebrew Bible. It conveys the idea of spending time thinking about the details of a matter. We might use it today to describe the care with which a stamp collector joyfully and carefully arranges the pages of his stamp book to make his prize collection more attractive. It would be used of a gardener who enthusiastically extracts every weed from his flower bed and fertilizes everything so that it will be green and beautiful.

Christians are told in Psalm 37:4 to show such devotion with their spiritual lives. We ought to take the same interest in the things of God that we would take with anything else that gives us pleasure. God commands that we delight in Him. To some people, the command seems utterly impossible, because today delight is perceived as an emotional issue. How can you be commanded to feel a certain way?

But Psalm 37:4 is not a command to emote; it is a command to act. God made us; He knows better than we that emotions do not do our bidding. He also knows that actions and emotions are tied together with bands of iron. Our emotional attachments to people should not come primarily because of the way they have behaved toward us, but *because of the way we have behaved toward them*. Though we cannot choose to emote, we can choose to behave.

God wants us to engage in those activities that will move our affections in His direction. He wants us to do what is right and constructive, because He knows that after a while our emotions will follow our actions. He wants us to spend time with Him, because that is part of what draws people together.

It works that way in every realm. "Nothing propinks like propinquity," the old adage says. *Propinquity* is a fancy word with an important meaning: being in close proximity or relationship. Nearness creates attraction. Couples become romantically attracted in part because they spend so much time together. The passing of time in each other's presence gives them an appreciation of each other.

The same principle works on a spiritual level. When you take a deep interest in your relationship to God, God becomes dear to you. That makes it even easier to continue to pursue the relationship further, and one day you look around and what God promises in Psalm 37:4 has become your experience. He has given you the desires of your heart, and you no longer are concerned for your emotional state with respect to Him. It is taking care of itself.

So why don't more people do it? Why don't more people make the simple choice to delight in the Lord—to do those activities that promote their spiritual lives—and allow Him the opportunity to return to them the desires of their hearts? One answer is *impatience*. Notice how Psalm 37 begins: "Do not fret because of evildoers, nor be envious of the workers of iniquity. For they shall soon be cut down like the grass, and wither as the green herb" (verses 1–2). Why begin a psalm like this? Because one of the persistent problems people run up against when it comes to delighting oneself in the Lord is the matter of the prosperity of those who do *not* delight themselves in Him.

The beginning and end of Psalm 37, as well as many verses in between, focus on this problem. The wicked *do* prosper, at least for a season. It is clear that David had thought it through. He knew how other people behaved, and he knew his own heart. Thus he wrote:

> Wait on the Lord, and keep His way, and He shall exalt you to inherit the land; when the wicked are cut off, you shall see it. I have seen the wicked in great power, and spreading himself like a native green tree. Yet he passed away, and behold, he was no more; indeed I sought him, but he could not be found. (vv. 34–36)

David said, in effect, if you can wait patiently for the Lord to act, you will discover that evildoers don't really prosper in the end. At the moment it might seem like it, but it's just a matter of time before matters are set aright. Their prosperity is fleeting. The success of those who delight in the Lord continues.

Another barrier to delighting in the Lord is *unbelief*. I am not referring to the unbelief of unbelievers, but to the unbelief of believers. (Did you follow that?) People who are outside the Christian faith usually do not spend time combing the Scriptures to make themselves aware of such incentives as Psalm 37:4. But Christians often exhibit unbelief over certain Bible promises. We frankly doubt the veracity of a statement that promises the desires of our hearts, even though we would never say that aloud or share our skepticism with our closest friend. We just ignore it, to our loss.

We naturally think that the opposite of delighting in the Lord is being sad; but the threat to delight in Psalm 37 is not sorrow, it is anger—the anger of the person who looks around him and sees what people are apparently getting away with. For example, the psalm insists: "Rest in the Lord, and wait patiently for Him; do not fret because of him who prospers in his way, because of the man who brings wicked schemes to pass. Cease from anger, and forsake wrath; do not fret—it only causes harm" (Psalm 37:7–8). If you spend a large part of your life fretting, you will not be able to delight in the Lord.

I know nothing that is a poorer recommendation of Christ than an angry Christian. That is why delighting yourself in the Lord is such a critical part of responding to Him. Until you can do that, you could be carrying around an anger that actually will deny everything you are professing as a believer. Having your heart in a state of calmness at all times is the best antidote for dealing with whatever is wrong with the world around you. Make no mistake about it; plenty is wrong. But being angry and fretting don't help. Delighting in the Lord does. It may not fix what's wrong with the world, but it will help you. It will remind you that you have resources more powerful than your troubles, and that there is Someone who cares for you. Additionally, you honor Him when you display an awareness that He is with you.

THE RESPONSE OF THE CARING BELIEVER

As God brings your own heart toward maturity and as you use meditation as one resource, you will become increasingly concerned with those matters which concern Him. Your prayer life will be changed as a result. Supplication—the bringing of requests to Him for yourself and others—is the response of the caring, transformed believer.

When we read Psalm 37:4 with its promise of gaining the desires of our hearts, we suspect that it has a catch. It does. If you delight yourself in the Lord, your desires are going to change. You will have a different list of "all that you could ever want" after you delight in Him for a while, and your prayer life will reflect the changes.

People are nonetheless afraid of those changes. They don't always believe that God has their best interests at heart. The apostle Paul anticipated this problem in Romans 8:32 when he wrote, "He who did not spare His own Son, but delivered Him up for us all, how shall He not with Him also freely give us all things?" How, indeed! God already gave the best anyone could ever give. How can we wonder that the things that He offers us will be in any way inferior or serve to make us unhappy people?

When we begin to realize how spiritually rich we are in Christ, we will want to take advantage of the wealth in our family. We will ask God to do still more wonderful things for us and for others. We will honor Him by requesting great acts of kindness and mercy which He alone can perform. Our prayer lives will reflect a consciousness of God's glorious power and our concern for people who need His goodness. A vigorous prayer life is the outgrowth of realizing God's truth and reflecting upon it.

THE RESPONSE OF THE DETERMINED BELIEVER

No one can meditate on the truth of God for long without realizing the importance of obedience. During our times of meditation we are better able and ought to make important decisions about new courses of action, new directions. If God's Word alerts us to areas of our lives that need changing—and it invariably will— then resolving to behave differently is part of the process. Making plans is part of meditation. Most people aren't serious about doing things differently until they have thought through how they will do so.

Of course, just making plans, as we all know from sad experience, accomplishes little. When all is said and done, more is usually said than done. Just because you have made a decision to obey God in a particular area does not guarantee that you will. But unless you have made that decision to obey, you almost certainly won't. A commitment is simply a set of decisions made in advance. When you are committed, you don't regard a biblical command as an invitation to open negotiations. There is no decision to be made.

Obedience is not an optional part of meditation. It is the reason why meditation exists in the first place. God's command to Joshua specified this: "This Book of the Law shall not depart from your mouth, but you shall meditate in it day and night, *that you may observe to do* according to all that is written in it" (Joshua 1:8, italics added). Moses told Israel, "Set your hearts on all the words which I testify among you today, which you shall command your children *to be careful to observe*—all the words of this law" (Deuteronomy 32:46, italics added).

More than anything else, failure to respond in obedience will destroy your experience of meditation. Refusal to do what pleases God will throw cold water all over your intentions to meditate. As D. L. Moody often said, "This Book will keep you from sin, or sin will keep you from this Book."

When I entered seminary in 1967, I was a young man with great intentions, but untested. In the course of my study I came to that penetrating question of the Lord Jesus: "If you have not been faithful in the unrighteous mammon, who will commit to your trust the true riches?" (Luke 16:11). Until this time, my own use of mammon (money) could hardly be described as "faithful." I paid my bills, but my giving was spotty and haphazard. The more I thought about the Lord's question, the more uncomfortable I became.

There ensued a period of personal struggle as I sought to come to grips with what God was looking for from me. I tried to explain things to Him: "But Lord, I'm just a poor seminarian. I have so little. Shouldn't I be considered a special case?" No amount of spiritual legerdemain, however, would erase Luke 16:11. I was supposedly headed for responsibility of the most exalted kind: to have a church of God's people entrusted to my pastoral care. I had to face the fact that my unfaithfulness in the area of giving might well disqualify me from such a position. So, with no small amount of trepidation I began to be systematic in giving a significant portion of my income to the Lord.

No, I didn't become wealthy as a result. Frankly, there were plenty of struggles. But my mind and heart were—and still are—at rest in the knowledge that I responded honestly toward the Word of God. And God did, in due time, give me "true riches" in the form of a group of people who wanted to know Christ and obey His Word.

MEDITATIONS IN HIS WORD

Realize

Read Luke 14:25–33.

Retain

Memorize Luke 14:26.

Reflect

1. If the reference to hating parents in verse 26 cannot be true in an absolute sense (Ephesians 6:1–3, for one passage, would argue against it), the Lord must be speaking in relative terms. What kind of situation might call for turning away from a parent's counsel or wishes in order to remain Christ's disciple?

2. *Disciple* is a word with both narrow and broad meanings in the New Testament. Its broader meaning is *believer*, as in Acts 6:1. What is its narrower meaning based on this passage?

3. In what sense must a disciple hate his own soul or life?

Respond

1. Be absolutely honest with God and yourself and evaluate your qualifications as a disciple in the sense mentioned in the passage.

2. Does it make sense to hold back in any respect from a total loyalty and devotion to Christ?

3. Think of some people you could influence in the direction of discipleship. What can you do to make it happen? What will you do?

[Senior demon Screwtape to junior demon Wormwood:]
Work hard, then, on the disappointment or anti-climax which is
certainly coming to the patient during his first few weeks as a
churchman. The Enemy allows this disappointment to occur on
the threshold of every human endeavour. It occurs when the boy
who has been enchanted in the nursery by Stories from the
Odyssey buckles down to really learning Greek. It occurs when
lovers have got married and begin the real task of learning to live
together. In every department of life it marks the transition from
dreaming aspiration to laborious doing. The Enemy takes this
risk because He has a curious fantasy of making all these disgust-
ing little human vermin into what He calls His "free" lovers and
servants—"sons" is the word He uses, with His inveterate love of
degrading the whole spiritual world by unnatural liaisons with
the two-legged animals. Desiring their freedom, He therefore re-
fuses to carry them, by their mere affections and habits, to any of
the goals which He sets before them: He leaves them to "do it on
their own." And there lies our opportunity. But also, remember,
there lies our danger. If once they get through this initial dryness
successfully, they become much less dependent on emotion and
therefore much harder to tempt.

—C. S. Lewis

CHAPTER 10

Rebuking the Soul

During May, 1752, Robert Robinson went to hear open-air British evangelist George Whitefield, and the teenager put his trust in Christ. Over the next four decades, Robinson served the Lord with distinction in the ministry of several churches. His books were discussed in the houses of Parliament and his ministry was widely known. His most enduring legacy to the Christian church, however, is a hymn. It begins, "Come thou Fount of every blessing, tune my heart to sing thy grace; streams of mercy, never ceasing, call for songs of loudest praise." It became very popular in his lifetime and remains a favorite hymn of thousands.

During one period of his life, however, Robinson went through a time of sin and estrangement from God. He became a living illustration of the line in the third verse of his own hymn, which reads, "Prone to wander, Lord, I feel it, prone to leave the God I love." Trying after some time to take his mind off his troubles, he set out on a vacation trip. Along the way he came to share a coach with a young woman who engaged him in a spiritual discussion. She explained how she had recently received Christ and how the hymn known as "Come Thou Fount" had come to mean a great deal to her (she was unaware that she was speaking with its author).

Robinson tried to divert the conversation into other channels, but she innocently continued her testimony. Eventually God's conviction struck his heart, and he began to weep. With tears streaming down his cheeks, he said, "I am the man who wrote that hymn many years ago." Though the woman was greatly surprised, she was wise too. She reminded him that the "streams of mercy" he wrote about were still flowing.

THE CORRECTING ACTION OF MEDITATION

Because we are all "prone to wander," meditation necessarily includes self-correction. It is glorious when a wanderer returns to Jesus Christ. It is still better not to stray. The self-rebuke of meditation helps in both cases. The Spirit of God uses the Word to bring conviction to our hearts. Whether we are facing temptation or have already yielded to it, God's Word points us in the right direction.

Unfortunately, we don't always listen. The Corinthian church once fell into the horrible practice of abusing the Lord's Table. When the church met, those with food would begin eating without regard to whether their brothers and sisters were present to honor the Lord with them—or even had food at all. Instead of the time being a period of sharing and reflection on the Lord's death, it turned into an exhibition of gluttony and drunkenness.

As you might imagine, the Lord Jesus was grieved. Even so, it took some time for His discipline to unfold. The apostle Paul had to explain it to the Corinthians, in fact, since they had become spiritually dense. He wrote, "For this reason many are weak and sick among you, and many sleep" (1 Corinthians 11:30). Some in the church were merely experiencing weakness, but others were ill, and many had died—all because they had despised the central institution of the Christian church. The apostle then added the hopeful dictum: "If we would judge ourselves, we would not be judged" (1 Corinthians 11:31). Divine discipline only comes when we refuse to take the responsibility for self-rebuke and correction. A regular experience of meditation in His Word will keep us in touch with Him and stimulate us to engage in proper self-judgment.

Every generation seems to possess its own provocations to

waywardness. Many Christians today have imbibed enough of the elixir of the age to struggle in particular with their emotions. "God doesn't want me to be unhappy" has become the motto of a whole generation of unstable believers. And many are told that to deny their emotional inclinations makes them hypocrites.

GIVING ANSWERS TO OUR EMOTIONS

How can it be right to oppose one's emotions in order to do what is right? At least one answer appears in Psalm 42, where an emotionally spent servant of God recalls happier days and rebukes his soul for its sorrowful attitudes. His argument with himself, which spills over into Psalm 43, illustrates the kind of internal discussion that meditation often involves.

The psalm unveils the thinking of a person who takes responsibility for his own spiritual life. Here the focus is on turning away from discouragement. The psalmist's self-talk is not designed to accuse himself of doing wrong, but to straighten out his attitude, which has fallen into an unjustifiable sadness.

The psalmist says to himself in 42:5, "Why are you cast down, O my soul? And why are you disquieted within me? Hope in God, for I shall yet praise Him for the help of His countenance." I appreciate the utter realism of the Bible. Here you do not see a man who is above the fray. The psalmist is a person of deep spirituality with an intense heart's desire to know God (see vv. 1–2). Nonetheless, he knows his own vulnerability.

So what does a godly person do who is discouraged? Does he engage in self-hypnosis? Does he try autosuggestivism, the sort that Emile Coué made popular back at the turn of the century: "Every day, in every way, I'm getting better and better"?

No, he simply recognizes that there is spiritual bedrock beneath his feet. He may have hit bottom, but the bottom is solid. How does he know this? Because he has a history with God. He knows from happy experience that God is faithful. He has reason to be confident that this occasion will not prove to be an exception. Today, too many Christians seem ready to ask God, "What have You done for me lately?"

Self-correction often boils down to overcoming an emotion-caused resistance. Believers have to cope with this more today than ever. At the time this psalm was written, if you had said to the psalmist, "You're going to have to get control of your emotions, my friend, and make sure that your heart is inclined in God's direction. Don't let your discouragement move you into doing something foolish or immoral," he would have said, "Of course."

A modern person might say instead, "Oh, no, I can't go against my emotions." Today, when Christians do what is wrong, they almost always attempt to use their emotional state to justify sinful behavior. Take, for example, the woman who says, "I am not happy with my husband. God doesn't want me to be sad the rest of my life." This, in her mind, justifies, or at least mitigates, her decision to leave her husband, though he may love her and desperately want her to stay.

"I just don't love my wife anymore" is likewise the refrain of the wayward husband. The subtle implication is, "Since my emotions are no longer at the fever pitch they once were, this marriage really ought to end." Then there is the Christian who says, "I just wasn't in the mood to pray." For him, prayer would be improper without the proper emotional ambience.

He would sympathize with the employee who groans, "I didn't feel like going to work today." He doesn't mean that he was ill, just that he lacked enthusiasm for the work. Letting his emotions rule his behavior has cost him his integrity—and may cost him his job.

During meditation in the Word we regularly meet people who did what was right even when their natural inclinations pushed them toward what was expedient. They ruled their decisions with or without the assistance of their emotions.

SOME BIBLICAL FACTS ABOUT EMOTIONS

In view of the dangers of letting sin get its head in this realm, it may be worthwhile to consider some fundamental teachings of Scripture about emotions.

Emotions Change

Emotions change frequently and quickly. Mark records a dramatic incident during Jesus' ministry:

Meditation
Close-up
Dealing with Deceptive Emotions

Believers who meditate become increasingly realistic. They recognize where the true spiritual dangers lie within themselves, particularly in dealing with their emotions. They recognize that those emotions often pose serious threats to their spiritual growth. A healthy form of self-rebuke will take place, for self-rebuke is part of meditation. Such self-talk requires:

- Understanding the facts of what the Bible has to say about emotions: their variability, their true nature, and their dangers.
- Information about how emotions relate to hypocrisy.
- A resolve to be calm and to consult the Word before acting.
- A commitment not to abandon during dark times the truth that God's Word has taught you in the light.

[Jesus] came to the house. . . and saw a tumult and those who wept and wailed loudly. When He came in, He said to them, "Why make this commotion and weep? The child is not dead, but sleeping." And they laughed Him to scorn. . . . Then He took the child by the hand, and said to her, . . . "Little girl, I say to you, arise." Immediately the girl arose and walked, for she was twelve years of age. And they were overcome with great amazement. (Mark 5:38–42)

Here we see a crowd move from extreme sorrow to scornful laughter to utter amazement all in the course of a few short minutes. The devil knows how to make use of our vulnerability in this area. He convinces us when we are on the mountaintop that the mountaintop is the norm. Then, when we fall into the valley, our conscience whips us with the question, "Why aren't you on the mountaintop? Real Christians are always on top of things."

Even worse, we conclude that because we are sorrowful right now, we will be sorrowful for the foreseeable future. The Psalms put the lie to it. In about a third of the 150 psalms, the psalmist at one point or another acknowledges that he is either depressed or discouraged or frustrated with something. The psalmist uses self-rebuke in Psalm 42 to deal with that. "I will yet praise Him," he says. "I won't be in this hole indefinitely. There's an end to it."

Emotions Are Consequences, Not Virtues

We haven't achieved anything by emoting, in spite of society's insistence to the contrary. If we are really stirred up by romantic love, for example, the culture congratulates and says we are virtuous. But the fact that we are thrilled to see a person during the courtship doesn't ensure that the marriage will be a good one.

I have tried to tell all the couples that I have married through the years that premarital counseling (in spite of the name) is not to prepare them to be married.

Nothing can make them ready for that.

Premarital counseling will merely make them less unready. I try to tell them that they are going to learn things about themselves by being married that will not make them very happy. They are going to experience moments of deep discouragement when they come face-to-face with their own self-centeredness as well as their mate's. That happens to everybody. If emotions were virtues, none of this could be fixed. We would merely say to our spouses, "My emotions aren't where they should be. It's up to you to make things right." Come to think of it, many couples make that exact mistake.

Emotions Make Us Vulnerable to Falsehood

The mind is prone to believe exaggerations when we are in emotional extremes. In sorrow we tell ourselves: *I'm incompetent. I'll never amount to anything.* In joy, a young man declares silently (and perhaps aloud): *My excitement about this woman will never end.* In grief, a woman thinks: *I'll never be happy again.*

In Psalm 42, the writer faces an additional complication. Two groups of people are making his life difficult. The external enemies have driven him into exile across the Jordan. Then there are the people with him whose mission in life seems to be to discourage him. Their chorus is: "Where is your God?" Discouragement doesn't always come from outside the camp.

Emotions Are Morally Neutral

God invented human emotions. They are neither virtues nor vices, and they can never be used with validity to excuse sinful behavior. During your meditation, when you come face-to-face with a text that requires you to do battle with your inclinations, remember that. Emotions are simply part of our humanity. Christ experienced them all, and yet did not sin. For example, Mark 14:34 tells us that in the garden of Gethsemane, Jesus told the disciples, "My soul is exceedingly sorrowful, even to death." The impending separation from the Father was so overwhelming that the sorrow from it was almost enough to kill Him by itself. Yet in experiencing this sorrow, He did not sin.

Jesus knew grief; John 11:35 records how He wept before the grave of His dear friend Lazarus. He experienced joy. Luke 10:21 tells us that "In that hour Jesus rejoiced in the Spirit and said, 'I praise You, Father, Lord of heaven and earth.'" The Lord Jesus even experienced anger as He drove the money changers out of the temple precincts. Mark 3:5 explains that Jesus, in the synagogue at Capernaum, was upset at the Jewish leaders' indifference toward human need: He "looked around at them with anger."

We nearly always will need to engage in some healthy self-talk during meditation, just as the psalmist did, to keep from doing things we will regret, or—much more commonly—failing to do the things that we know we should, but which our emotions resist.

CONFRONTING THE INNER PERSON

Today it is fashionable to abandon God's ways in the interest of being free from hypocrisy. But hypocrisy is pretending to be something you are not. Hypocrisy would be pretending to be joyful in the pursuit of God's will while crushed with sorrow. When Abraham walked with Isaac toward the place where he would offer up his beloved son, you may be confident that he was not whistling a happy tune.

Doing What Is Right

Doing what is right, even if it is contrary to my feelings, is simply obedience. No display should be made of how much fun it is to oppose our emotions and obey God. Psalm 42 contains no hypocrisy, merely a recognition that the psalmist's sorrowful condition will not last, providing an anchor against despair based on that fact. C. S. Lewis recognized the folly of consulting feelings when he wrote:

> Faith . . . is the art of holding on to things your reason has once accepted, in spite of your changing moods. For moods will change, whatever view your reason takes. I know that by experience. Now that I am a Christian I do have moods in which the whole thing looks very improbable: but when I was an atheist I had moods in which Christianity looked terribly probable. This rebellion of your moods against your real self is going to come anyway. That is why Faith is such a necessary virtue: unless you teach your moods "where they get off," you can never be either a sound Christian or even a sound atheist, but just a creature dithering to and fro, with its beliefs really dependent on the weather and the state of its digestion.[1]

An Example: David at Ziklag

In the days before Saul's death, David was a fugitive from his own land. He and his band of men had become apparent allies of the Philistines and lived in the remote southern part of Israel near Philistia at a wide spot in the road called Ziklag. The town had been given to David as a reward for services by the Philistine king Achish. (I imagine David was tempted to give it back when he saw it. After a while, however, it was home.)

He and his men returned to Ziklag one day to discover that Amalekite raiders had plundered it and kidnapped their wives and children. Nothing was left. All their valuables were gone. All their families were gone.

David and the people who were with him were crushed. Here they were doing what was right, waiting for the day when David would be lifted to the throne of his nation, and they had lost the one anchor in their lives—their families. When they saw what had happened, David and his men wept profusely: so much, in fact, that they no longer had the strength to weep any more. After they ran out of energy to grieve, everyone took stock of the situation. The people concluded that it was all David's fault. He had brought them to this place. He was to blame.

There was even talk of killing him. "Now David was greatly distressed, for the people spoke of stoning him, because the soul of all the people was grieved, every man for his sons and his daughters. But David strengthened himself in the Lord his God" (1 Samuel 30:6). David engaged in some serious self-talk.

The very first thing he did was *to go to the Word of God*. He called for Abiathar the priest and asked him to bring the priestly ephod. Worn over the chest, the ephod included the Urim and Thummim, the "Lights and Perfections" (Exodus 28:1–30; Numbers 27:21), which were a means (not entirely understood today) of discovering the will of God. David inquired of the Lord and asked whether he should go after the Philistines, and God said that he should. He eventually recaptured everything; but none of it would have been possible if he had given in, as everyone else had done, to his emotional state.

We have no guarantees from God that our personal circumstances will always be excellent. Therefore, we shift our hope from the circumstances to the One behind the circumstances.

By the way, there is no virtue in trying to change your emotions directly. There is no point in saying, "I'm now going to proceed to be joyful and I'm going to feel wonderful." That is not self-correction, but denial. Put your hope in God, as the psalmist did, and let your emotions take care of themselves. Where He is, everything is calm.

The best feature about hoping in God is that no circumstances exist which can defeat it. God is the same every day. We don't have an ephod to consult to know exactly what the will of God is for a particular situation, but we don't need one. We have a complete Bible, which tells us what God is like every day. It tells us of His commitment to us, as exhibited in His Son coming here to die for us. Jesus Christ hanging on the cross is God's full and complete answer to the question of whether He loves us or not. If that won't convince us, nothing will. We need to remind ourselves of that unalterable proof that He cares. We may be on the bottom from time to time—but the bottom is solid.

MEDITATIONS IN HIS WORD

Realize

Read Psalm 42.

Retain

Memorize Psalm 42:5.

Reflect

1. In verses 3 and 10, the psalmist's opponents belittle him with a taunt: "Where is your God?" The question assumes that the psalmist is openly on the record before his neighbors as hoping in God, yet at the time of his ridicule, the Lord seems distant. To what extent could people you know hurl this broadside at you? To what extent have they?

2. Contrast the way things were in former times (verse 4). What role does corporate worship have in keeping you in a proper frame of mind?

3. Though the Lord had not forgotten the psalmist, it appeared that He had. Are the questions of verse 9 entirely consumed with self-interest, or does the psalmist regret the damage done to God's cause by his own discomfort?

4. Do you periodically remind yourself of your confidence in God's ultimate rescue of you when you are sorrowful (Psalm 42:5, 11)? Is this kind of statement realism or wishful thinking?

Respond

1. Do you often use the state of your emotions as a justification for sins of commission or omission? If so, confess your behavior to God.

2. Have you ever fallen prey to the fallacy that the person who knows God well must understand what He is doing at all times? Ask God to help you be comfortable

with His sovereign ordering of your life.

3. Is there a context (neighborhood, school, work, home) in which you need to go on record as being a believer in Jesus Christ? If so, ask Him to give you courage to do so, and to give you wisdom in knowing how and when to express your faith.

Complacency is a deadly foe of all spiritual growth. Acute desire must be present or there will be no manifestation of Christ to His people. He waits to be wanted. Too bad that with many of us He waits so long, so very long, in vain.

—A. W. Tozer

Getting to Know God

Let me remind you that the basic pattern of meditation is quite simple:

- Realize the truth of God (through reading and study).
- Reflect on the truth of God .
- Respond to the truth of God (in worship, prayer, and obedience).

If you plan to meditate intermittently throughout the day—and you must, to receive the maximum benefits from the process—you will need to add another step near the beginning of the process, and that is

- Retain the truth of God (through memorization).

There is nothing particularly exotic or difficult about meditation. Just about any Christian who wants to meditate can do so.

There is nothing magical about it, either. Meditation will not instantly undo the consequences of sinful patterns that have taken a lifetime to build. It will, however, help you to learn to cope with those consequences and to replace those patterns. Think of meditation as a trowel that God wields as He does some interior reconstruction. He works brick by brick; and if given the tool frequently enough, He will build something significant.

At its heart, however, meditation is simply a means of knowing God, and no one can know Him and not be the better for it. I commend you to your journey of meditation by relating an event which took place during the Reformation era. An admirer approached Martin Luther and asked him to autograph his New Testament. Luther did so and added some words of encouragement.

Luther called the admirer's attention to the antagonistic religious leaders in John's gospel who challenged Jesus by asking disdainfully, "Who are You?" The Lord's response was, "Just what I have been saying to you from the beginning" (John 8:25). Then Luther wrote:

> They . . . desire to know who [Jesus] is and not to regard what he says, while he desires them first to listen; then they will know who he is. The rule is: Listen and allow the Word to make the beginning; then the knowing will nicely follow. If, however, you do not listen, you will never know anything. For it is decreed: God will not be seen, known or comprehended except through his Word alone.[1]

Getting to know God is a lifelong pursuit. It requires a heart for learning and waiting, and it always requires that we look foremost in His Word. Meditate on the Scriptures. As you do, you will participate in the ongoing and rewarding process of knowing God up close.

ENDNOTES

Introduction: A Sure Thing

1. George Barna, *What Americans Believe* (Ventura, Calif.: Regal, 1991), 288.
2. Ibid., 291.
3. Gary L. W. Johnson, "Does Theology Still Matter?" in *The Coming Evangelical Crisis,* John H. Armstrong, gen. ed. (Chicago: Moody, 1996), 61.
4. Quoted in Michael P. Green, ed., *Illustrations for Biblical Preaching* (Grand Rapids: Baker, 1989), 18.
5. Walter Moberly, *The Crisis in the University* (London: SCM, 1949), 52.
6. Barna, *What Americans Believe,* 217–19.
7. As cited in Howard G. Hendricks and William D. Hendricks, *Living by the Book* (Chicago: Moody, 1991), 10.
8. Barna, *What Americans Believe,* 204–206.
9. Based on title and publisher. Most books on meditation are openly slanted toward eastern religions (Hinduism or Buddhism), or the modern (you should pardon the expression) incarnations of eastern religion, transcendental meditation, and the New Age movement.

Chapter 1: What Meditation Is

1. The ad was placed in the *Times* on April 10, 1940, by Simon & Schuster to advertise Mortimer Adler's *How to Read a Book.*
2. J. I. Packer, *Knowing God* (Downers Grove, Ill.: InterVarsity, 1973), 18–19.
3. As quoted in *The Biblical Illustrator,* June 1989, 414–34.
4. *Autobiography of George Mueller,* compiled by Fred Bergen (London: J. Nisbet Co., 1906), 152–154; as quoted in John Piper, *Desiring God* (Portland: Multnomah, 1986), 127–29.

Chapter 2: What Meditation Isn't

1. Adapted from a story in James S. Hewett, ed., *Parables,* February 1987 [computer file service] (Saratoga Press, in Saratoga, Calif.).
2. Richard Foster, *Celebration of Discipline* (San Francisco: Harper & Row, 1978), 14.
3. Ibid.
4. Ibid., 17.
5. Ibid., 14, 19, 23.
6. Ibid., 27–28.
7. Ibid., 18–19.
8. Charles C. Ryrie, *Basic Theology* (Wheaton, Ill.: Victor, 1986), 116.

Chapter 3: The Motive for Meditation

1. Blaise Pascal, *Pensees,* A. J. Krailsheimer, trans. (New York: Penguin, 1966), 425.
2. A. W. Tozer, *Men Who Met God* (Camp Hill, Penn.: Christian Publications, 1986), 84.

Chapter 4: What Meditation Can Do for You

1. The Hebrew word *hokmah*, commonly rendered "wisdom," is actually translated "skill" in modern versions of passages like Exodus 35:35 and 1 Kings 7:14.
2. Derek Kidner, *Psalms 1–72: An Introduction and Commentary on Books I and II of the Psalms* (Leicester, England: InterVarsity, 1973), 48.
3. George E. Ladd in *Perspectives on the World Christian Movement: A Reader,* Ralph D. Winter and Steven Hawthorne, eds. (Pasadena, Calif.: William Carey Library, 1981), 66.
4. Glenn E. Meyers, "Think About It!" *Discipleship Journal,* July/August 1997, 104.
5. Lewis W. Spitz, ed., *Luther's Works,* as cited in "How to Study Theology," *Christianity Today,* 4 October 1993, 100.
6. Ibid.
7. Ibid., 96.
8. John D. Woodbridge, ed., *Renewing Your Mind in a Secular World* (Chicago: Moody, 1985), 25.
9. Paul Meier, *Meditating for Success* (Richardson, Tex.: Today Publishers, 1985), 8.
10. Ibid.
11. R. Kent Hughes, "Preaching: God's Word to the Church Today," in John H. Armstrong, gen. ed., *The Coming Evangelical Crisis* (Chicago: Moody, 1996), 94–95.

Chapter 5: The Substance of Meditation

1. Arthur Conan Doyle, "The Naval Treaty," in *The Original Illustrated Sherlock Holmes* (Secaucus, N.J.: Castle Books, 1981), 313.
2. Paul Brand and Philip Yancey, *Fearfully & Wonderfully Made: A Surgeon Looks at the Human and Spiritual Body* (Grand Rapids: Zondervan, 1980), 45–46.
3. Ibid., 46n.
4. This story is adapted from Leslie Flynn, *Come Alive with Illustrations!* (Grand Rapids: Baker, 1988), 139–40.

Chapter 6: Seeking God's Truth in the Word

1. As quoted in Leslie Flynn, *Your Inner You* (Wheaton, Ill.: Victor, 1984), 48.
2. Irving L. Jensen, *How to Profit from Bible Reading* (Chicago: Moody, 1985), 44–49.
3. Howard G. Hendricks and William D. Hendricks, *Living by the Book* (Chicago: Moody, 1991), 141–70. Those who want more in-depth teaching on methods of Bible study could hardly do better than this volume.
4. Ibid., 221–50.
5. This is clearly the case during his Palestinian sojourn. Abraham is sometimes asserted to be a city dweller at his call, but this is based on a dubious (in my judgment) identification of Ur of the Chaldees with the Ur of Sumer.

Chapter 7: Retaining God's Truth

1. Howard Rutledge and Phyllis Rutledge, *In the Presence of Mine Enemies* (Old Tappan, N.J.: Revell, 1973), 34.
2. Leslie Flynn, *Your Inner You* (Wheaton, Ill.: Victor, 1984), 55.
3. "Personal Glimpses," *Reader's Digest,* March 1993, 112.
4. Charles R. Swindoll, *Three Steps Forward, Two Steps Back* (Nashville: Thomas Nelson, 1980), 100–101.

Chapter 8: Reflecting on God's Truth

1. Dave Barry, "Rack Record," *Lafayette Journal and Courier,* 26 June 1995, B1.
2. Quoted in Glenn E. Myers, "Think About It!" *Discipleship Journal,* July/August 1997, 104.

3. *Bible Characters from the New Testament* (Grand Rapids: Zondervan, 1967), 45.

4. Norman Vincent Peale, *This Incredible Century* (Wheaton, Ill.: Tyndale, 1991), 111–12.

Chapter 9: Responding to God's Truth

1. C. S. Lewis, *Mere Christianity* (New York: Macmillan, 1943), 10.

Chapter 10: Rebuking the Soul

1. C. S. Lewis, *Mere Christianity* (New York: Macmillan, 1943), 123–24.

Conclusion: Getting to Know God

1. James Montgomery Boice, *Standing on the Rock* (Wheaton, Ill.: Tyndale, 1984), 27.